6. Enter your class ID code to join a class.

IF YOU HAVE A CLASS CODE FROM YOUR TEACHER

a. Enter your class code and click | Next |

b. Once you have joined a class, you will be able to use the Discussion Board and Email tools.

c. To enter this code later, choose **Join a Class**.

IF YOU DO NOT HAVE A CLASS CODE

a. If you do not have a class ID code, click | Skip |

b. You do not need a class ID code to use *iQ Online*.

c. To enter this code later, choose **Join a Class**.

7. Review registration information and click Log In. Then choose your book. Click **Activities** to begin using *iQ Online*.

IMPORTANT

- After you register, the next time you want to use *iQ Online*, go to www.iQOnlinePractice.com and log in with your email address and password.
- The online content can be used for 12 months from the date you register.
- For help, please contact customer service: eltsupport@oup.com.

WHAT IS iQ ONLINE ?

All new activities provide essential skills **practice** and support.

Vocabulary and Grammar **games** immerse you in the language and provide even more practice.

Authentic, engaging **videos** generate new ideas and opinions on the Unit Question.

Go to the Media Center to download or stream all **student book audio**.

Use the **Discussion Board** to discuss the Unit Question and more.

Email encourages communication with your teacher and classmates.

Automatic grading gives immediate feedback and tracks progress.

Progress Reports show what you have mastered and where you still need more practice.

OXFORD
UNIVERSITY PRESS

198 Madison Avenue
New York, NY 10016 USA

Great Clarendon Street, Oxford, OX2 6DP, United Kingdom

Oxford University Press is a department of the University of Oxford.
It furthers the University's objective of excellence in research, scholarship,
and education by publishing worldwide. Oxford is a registered trade
mark of Oxford University Press in the UK and in certain other countries

Director, ELT New York: Laura Pearson
Head of Adult, ELT New York: Stephanie Karras
Publisher: Sharon Sargent
Managing Editor: Mariel DeKranis
Development Editor: Eric Zuarino
Executive Art and Design Manager: Maj-Britt Hagsted
Design Project Manager: Debbie Lofaso
Content Production Manager: Julie Armstrong
Senior Production Artist: Elissa Santos
Image Manager: Trisha Masterson
Image Editor: Liaht Ziskind
Production Coordinator: Brad Tucker

ISBN: 978 0 19 481902 2 Student Book 3 with iQ Online pack
ISBN: 978 0 19 481903 9 Student Book 3 as pack component
ISBN: 978 0 19 481802 5 iQ Online student website

Printed in China
This book is printed on paper from certified and well-managed sources.

ACKNOWLEDGEMENTS

*Although every effort has been made to trace and contact copyright holders before
publication, this has not been possible in some cases. We apologize for any apparent
infringement of copyright and if notified, the publisher will be pleased to rectify any
errors or omissions at the earliest opportunity.*

*The authors and publisher are grateful to those who have given permission to
reproduce the following extracts and adaptations of copyright material:*

p. 65 from "Living 'outside the box' - one escapee's TV-turn-off year" by
Stacey A. Teicher, *Christian Science Monitor*, April 27, 2005, http://www.
csmonitor.com/2005/0427/p09s02-coop.html. Adapted with permission
of Christian Science Monitor; p. 91 "In Defense of Advertising" from *The
Age of Persuasion*, CBC Radio One, Terry O'Reilly and Mike Tennant. Used
by permission; p. 108 from "Fear Factor: Success and Risk in Extreme
Sports" by Brian Handwerk, *National Geographic News*, July 8, 2004, http://
news.nationalgeographic.com. Used by permission of National Geographic
Creative; p. 116 "The Climb of My Life" from *The Climb of My Life: Scaling
Mountains with a Borrowed Heart* by Kelly Perkins. Copyright © 2007 Kelly
Perkins. Used by permission of the author; p. 169 adapted from "How to
make the biggest difference when giving to a charity" by Sarah Rich, et al.,
from *Canadian Living*, excerpted from *Worldchanging: A User's Guide for the 21st
Century*, edited by Alex Steffen.

Illustrations by: p. 13 Stuart Bradford; p. 30 Barb Bastian; p. 33 Karen Minot;
p. 39 Karen Minot (France); Inside Back Cover: Ivcandy/Getty Images/Bloom
Design/ Shutterstock.

*We would also like to thank the following for permission to reproduce the following
photographs*: Cover: Yongyut Kumsri/Shutterstock; Video Vocabulary
(used throughout the book): Oleksiy Mark / Shutterstock; p. 2 Zoonar/
WWW SHOCK CO /Age Fotostock; p. 3 Blue Jean Images/Corbis UK Ltd.
(businessman); p. 3 fotko/iStockphoto (vacancy); p. 3 Africa Studio/
Shutterstock (gifts); p. 4 Photodisc/Oxford University Press (cafe); p. 4
Blend Images/Alamy (businesswoman); p. 6 Betsie Van Der Meer/Getty
Images; p. 7 MIXA /Alamy; p. 13 Stockbyte/Oxford University Press; p. 28/29
Glow Cuisine/Getty Images; p. 32 California California/Alamy; p. 39
funkyfood London - Paul Williams/Alamy; p. 54 Tom Gilks/Alamy; p. 54/55
reznix/iStockphoto; p. 55 Zlatko Kostic/Getty Images (transparent); p. 55
Henrik5000/iStockphoto (3D cable); p. 58 Tobias Schwarz/Reuters/Corbis
UK Ltd.; p. 65 Tony Cordoza/Alamy; p. 66 Ethno Images, Inc. / Alamy; p. 80
Len Holsborg/Alamy; p. 80 OUP/rSnapshotPhotos (clouds); p. 80/81 UIG
via Getty Images/Getty Images; p. 81 Anthony Hatley/Alamy (subway);
p. 81 jonathansloane/iStockphoto (cowmobile); p. 82 Ilene MacDonald/
Alamy (colonel); p. 82 dmac/Alamy (billboard); p. 82 Howard Davies/
Alamy (climate); p. 82 Justin Kase z03z/Alamy (truck); p. 84 Ingram/Oxford
University Press; p. 91 Eric Audras/Getty Images; p. 104 Grey Adam/PA
Photos/ABACA/Newscom; p. 105 Lawrence Manning/Corbis UK Ltd. (pick);
p. 105 Bob Ingelhart/iStockphoto (climber); p. 106 Steve Glass/Alamy
(rockclimbing); p. 106 Adam Duckworth/Alamy (motocross); p. 106 IML
Image Group Ltd/Alamy (bungee); p. 106 Kadmy/Fotolia (painter); p. 106
imageBROKER/Alamy (skiing); p. 106 Bridget Besaw/Aurora Photos/Co/
Corbis UK Ltd. (logger); p. 106 Cultura Creative (RF)/Alamy (steelworker);
p. 106 Warren Palmer/Alamy (roofing); p. 106 Monty Rakusen/Cultura/
Corbis UK Ltd. (fishermen); p. 106 Philip Scalia/Alamy (tractor); p. 106
Thorsten Jochim/Getty Images (whitewater); p. 106 bikeriderlondon/
Shutterstock (mountaineer); p. 108 Krebs Hanns/Alamy; p. 117 Steven
Milne/Alamy; p. 130/131 Liz Mitchell/Demotix/Corbis UK Ltd.; p. 132
KAMARUL AKHIR/AFP/Getty Images (wheelchair); p. 132 Image Source/
Getty Images (mapreading); p. 132 Jochen Tack/Alamy (breakdown); p. 132
Ammentorp Photography/Alamy (pickpocket); p. 133 RayArt Graphics/
Alamy; p. 135 Inspirestock Inc./Alamy; p. 142 Scott Camazine/Alamy;
p. 158/159 AP Photo/PRNewsFoto/Heifer International; p. 160 JKlingebiel/
Shutterstock (lamb); p. 160 Photodisc/Oxford University Press (honeybee);
p. 160 Robert Fried/Alamy (silkworms); p. 160 Martin Ruegner/Getty
Images (chicks); p. 160 Stephen Dorey/Oxford University Press (goat);
p. 160 GWImages/Shutterstock (stationery); p. 162 Darren K. Fisher/
Shutterstock (graduation); p. 162 Jerod Harris/Heifer International (Birra);
p. 164 67photo/Alamy; p. 171 Trickle Up; p. 186 Shamukov Ruslan Itar-
Tass Photos/Newscom; p. 186 Mega Pixel/Shutterstock; p. 187 F1online
digitale Bildagentur GmbH/Alamy (Nobel); p. 187 B Calkins/Shutterstock
(APlus); p. 190 Glowimages/Getty Images (racecar); p. 190 Tee/LAT/Rex
Features (Formula1); p. 195 Photodisc/Oxford University Press; p. 196 Steve
Lindridge/Eye Ubiquitous/Corbis UK Ltd.; p. 202 Image Source/Oxford
University Press; Back Cover: mozcann/iStockphoto.

SHAPING learning TOGETHER

We would like to acknowledge the teachers from all over the world who participated in the development process and review of the Q series.

Special thanks to our *Q: Skills for Success* Second Edition Topic Advisory Board

Shaker Ali Al-Mohammad, Buraimi University College, Oman; **Dr. Asmaa A. Ebrahim**, University of Sharjah, U.A.E.; **Rachel Batchilder**, College of the North Atlantic, Qatar; **Anil Bayir**, Izmir University, Turkey; **Flora Mcvay Bozkurt**, Maltepe University, Turkey; **Paul Bradley**, University of the Thai Chamber of Commerce Bangkok, Thailand; **Joan Birrell-Bertrand**, University of Manitoba, MB, Canada; **Karen E. Caldwell**, Zayed University, U.A.E.; **Nicole Hammond Carrasquel**, University of Central Florida, FL, U.S.; **Kevin Countryman**, Seneca College of Applied Arts & Technology, ON, Canada; **Julie Crocker**, Arcadia University, NS, Canada; **Marc L. Cummings**, Jefferson Community and Technical College, KY, U.S.; **Rachel DeSanto**, Hillsborough Community College Dale Mabry Campus, FL, U.S.; **Nilüfer Ertürkmen**, Ege University, Turkey; **Sue Fine**, Ras Al Khaimah Women's College (HCT), U.A.E.; **Amina Al Hashami**, Nizwa College of Applied Sciences, Oman; **Stephan Johnson**, Nagoya Shoka Daigaku, Japan; **Sean Kim**, Avalon, South Korea; **Gregory King**, Chubu Daigaku, Japan; **Seran Küçük**, Maltepe University, Turkey; **Jonee De Leon**, VUS, Vietnam; **Carol Lowther**, Palomar College, CA, U.S.; **Erin Harris-MacLeod**, St. Mary's University, NS, Canada; **Angela Nagy**, Maltepe University, Turkey; **Huynh Thi Ai Nguyen**, Vietnam; **Daniel L. Paller**, Kinjo Gakuin University, Japan; **Jangyo Parsons**, Kookmin University, South Korea; **Laila Al Qadhi**, Kuwait University, Kuwait; **Josh Rosenberger**, English Language Institute University of Montana, MT, U.S.; **Nancy Schoenfeld**, Kuwait University, Kuwait; **Jenay Seymour**, Hongik University, South Korea; **Moon-young Son**, South Korea; **Matthew Taylor**, Kinjo Gakuin Daigaku, Japan; **Burcu Tezcan-Unal**, Zayed University, U.A.E.; **Troy Tucker**, Edison State College-Lee Campus, FL, U.S.; **Kris Vicca**, Feng Chia University, Taichung; **Jisook Woo**, Incheon University, South Korea; **Dunya Yenidunya**, Ege University, Turkey

UNITED STATES **Marcarena Aguilar**, North Harris College, TX; **Rebecca Andrade**, California State University North Ridge, CA; **Lesley Andrews**, Boston University, MA; **Deborah Anholt**, Lewis and Clark College, OR; **Robert Anzelde**, Oakton Community College, IL; **Arlys Arnold**, University of Minnesota, MN; **Marcia Arthur**, Renton Technical College, WA; **Renee Ashmeade**, Passaic County Community College, NJ; **Anne Bachmann**, Clackamas Community College, OR; **Lida Baker**, UCLA, CA; **Ron Balsamo**, Santa Rosa Junior College, CA; **Lori Barkley**, Portland State University, OR; **Eileen Barlow**, SUNY Albany, NY; **Sue Bartch**, Cuyahoga Community College, OH; **Lora Bates**, Oakton High School, VA; **Barbara Batra**, Nassau County Community College, NY; **Nancy Baum**, University of Texas at Arlington, TX; **Rebecca Beck**, Irvine Valley College, CA; **Linda Berendsen**, Oakton Community College, IL; **Jennifer Binckes Lee**, Howard Community College, MD; **Grace Bishop**, Houston Community College, TX; **Jean W. Bodman**, Union County College, NJ; **Virginia Bouchard**, George Mason University, VA; **Kimberley Briesch Sumner**, University of Southern California, CA; **Kevin Brown**, University of California, Irvine, CA; **Laura Brown**, Glendale Community College, CA; **Britta Burton**, Mission College, CA; **Allison L. Callahan**, Harold Washington College, IL; **Gabriela Cambiasso**, Harold Washington College, IL; **Jackie Campbell**, Capistrano Unified School District, CA; **Adele C. Camus**, George Mason University, VA; **Laura Chason**, Savannah College, GA; **Kerry Linder Catana**, Language Studies International, NY; **An Cheng**, Oklahoma State University, OK; **Carole Collins**, North Hampton Community College, PA; **Betty R. Compton**, Intercultural Communications College, HI; **Pamela Couch**, Boston University, MA; **Fernanda Crowe**, Intrax International Institute, CA; **Vicki Curtis**, Santa Cruz, CA; **Margo Czinski**, Washtenaw Community College, MI; **David Dahnke**, Lone Star College, TX; **Gillian M. Dale**, CA; **L. Dalgish**, Concordia College, MN; **Christopher Davis**, John Jay College, NY; **Sherry Davis**, Irvine University, CA; **Natalia de Cuba**, Nassau County Community College, NY; **Sonia Delgadillo**, Sierra College, CA; **Esmeralda Diriye**, Cypress College & Cal Poly, CA; **Marta O. Dmytrenko-Ahrabian**, Wayne State University, MI; **Javier Dominguez**, Central High School, SC; **Jo Ellen Downey-Greer**, Lansing Community College, MI; **Jennifer Duclos**, Boston University, MA; **Yvonne Duncan**, City College of San Francisco, CA; **Paul Dydman**, USC Language Academy, CA; **Anna Eddy**, University of Michigan-Flint, MI; **Zohan El-Gamal**, Glendale Community College, CA; **Jennie Farnell**, University of Connecticut, CT; **Susan Fedors**, Howard Community College, MD; **Valerie Fiechter**, Mission College, CA; **Ashley Fifer**, Nassau County Community College, NY; **Matthew Florence**, Intrax International Institute, CA; **Kathleen Flynn**, Glendale College, CA; **Elizabeth Fonsea**, Nassau County Community College, NY; **Eve Fonseca**, St. Louis Community College, MO; **Elizabeth Foss**, Washtenaw Community College, MI; **Duff C. Galda**, Pima Community College, AZ; **Christiane Galvani**, Houston Community College, TX; **Gretchen Gerber**, Howard Community College, MD; **Ray Gonzalez**, Montgomery College, MD; **Janet Goodwin**, University of California, Los Angeles, CA; **Alyona Gorokhova**, Grossmont College, CA; **John Graney**, Santa Fe College, FL; **Kathleen Green**, Central High School, AZ; **Nancy Hamadou**, Pima Community College-West Campus, AZ; **Webb Hamilton**, De Anza College, San Jose City College, CA; **Janet Harclerode**, Santa Monica Community College, CA; **Sandra Hartmann**, Language and Culture Center, TX; **Kathy Haven**, Mission College, CA; **Roberta Hendrick**, Cuyahoga Community College, OH; **Ginny Heringer**, Pasadena City College, CA; **Adam Henricksen**, University of Maryland, MD; **Carolyn Ho**, Lone Star College-CyFair, TX; **Peter Hoffman**, LaGuardia Community College, NY; **Linda Holden**, College of Lake County, IL; **Jana Holt**, Lake Washington Technical College, WA; **Antonio Iccarino**, Boston University, MA; **Gail Ibele**, University of Wisconsin, WI; **Nina Ito**, American Language Institute, CSU Long Beach, CA; **Linda Jensen**, UCLA, CA; **Lisa Jurkowitz**, Pima Community College, CA; **Mandy Kama**, Georgetown University, Washington, DC; **Stephanie Kasuboski**, Cuyahoga Community College, OH; **Chigusa Katoku**, Mission College, CA; **Sandra Kawamura**, Sacramento City College, CA; **Gail Kellersberger**, University of Houston-Downtown, TX; **Jane Kelly**, Durham Technical Community College, NC; **Maryanne Kildare**, Nassau County Community College, NY; **Julie Park Kim**, George Mason University, VA; **Kindra Kinyon**, Los Angeles Trade-Technical College, CA; **Matt Kline**, El Camino College, CA; **Lisa Kovacs-Morgan**, University of California, San Diego, CA; **Claudia Kupiec**, DePaul University, IL; **Renee La Rue**, Lone Star College-Montgomery, TX; **Janet Langon**, Glendale College, CA; **Lawrence Lawson**, Palomar College, CA; **Rachele Lawton**, The Community College of Baltimore County, MD; **Alice Lee**, Richland College, TX; **Esther S. Lee**, CSUF & Mt. SAC, CA; **Cherie Lenz-Hackett**, University of Washington, WA; **Joy Leventhal**, Cuyahoga Community College, OH; **Alice Lin**, UCI Extension, CA; **Monica Lopez**, Cerritos College, CA; **Dustin Lovell**, FLS International Marymount College, CA; **Carol Lowther**, Palomar College, CA; **Candace Lynch-Thompson**, North Orange County Community College District, CA; **Thi Thi Ma**, City College of San Francisco, CA; **Steve Mac Isaac**, USC Long Academy, CA; **Denise Maduli-Williams**, City College of San Francisco, CA; **Eileen Mahoney**, Camelback High School, AZ; **Naomi Mardock**, MCC-Omaha, NE; **Brigitte Maronde**, Harold Washington College, IL; **Marilyn Marquis**, Laposita College CA; **Doris Martin**, Glendale Community College; Pasadena City College, CA; **Keith Maurice**, University of Texas at Arlington, TX; **Nancy Mayer**, University of Missouri-St. Louis, MO; **Aziah McNamara**, Kansas State University, KS; **Billie McQuillan**, Education Heights, MN; **Karen Merritt**, Glendale Union High School District, AZ; **Holly Milkowart**, Johnson County Community College, KS; **Eric Moyer**, Intrax International Institute, CA; **Gino Muzzatti**, Santa Rosa Junior College, CA; **Sandra Navarro**, Glendale Community College, CA; **Than Nyeinkhin**, ELAC, PCC, CA; **William Nedrow**, Triton College, IL; **Eric Nelson**, University of Minnesota, MN; **Than Nyeinkhin**, ELAC, PCC, CA; **Nguyen Chanh**, Center for English as a Second Language at the University of Arizona, AZ; **Rhony Ory**, Ygnacio Valley High School, CA; **Paul Parent**, Montgomery College, MD; **Dr. Sumeeta Patnaik**, Marshall University, WV; **Oscar Pedroso**, Miami Dade College, FL; **Robin Persiani**, Sierra College, CA; **Patricia Prenz-Belkin**, Hostos Community College, NY; **Suzanne Powell**, University of Louisville, KY; **Jim Ranalli**, Iowa State University, IA; **Toni R. Randall**, Santa Monica College, CA; **Vidya Rangachari**, Mission College, CA; **Elizabeth Rasmussen**, Northern Virginia Community College, VA; **Lara Ravitch**, Truman College, IL;

Deborah Repasz, San Jacinto College, TX; Marisa Recinos, English Language Center, Brigham Young University, UT; Andrey Reznikov, Black Hills State University, SD; Alison Rice, Hunter College, NY; Jennifer Robles, Ventura Unified School District, CA; Priscilla Rocha, Clark County School District, NV; Dzidra Rodins, DePaul University, IL; Maria Rodriguez, Central High School, AZ; Josh Rosenberger, English Language Institute University of Montana, MT; Alice Rosso, Bucks County Community College, PA; Rita Rozzi, Xavier University, OH; Maria Ruiz, Victor Valley College, CA; Kimberly Russell, Clark College, WA; Stacy Sabraw, Michigan State University, MI; Irene Sakk, Northwestern University, IL; Deborah Sandstrom, University of Illinois at Chicago, IL; Jenni Santamaria, ABC Adult, CA; Shaeley Santiago, Ames High School, IA; Peg Sarosy, San Francisco State University, CA; Alice Savage, North Harris College, TX; Donna Schaeffer, University of Washington, WA; Karen Marsh Schaeffer, University of Utah, UT; Carol Schinger, Northern Virginia Community College, VA; Robert Scott, Kansas State University, KS; Suell Scott, Sheridan Technical Center, FL; Shira Seaman, Global English Academy, NY; Richard Seltzer, Glendale Community College, CA; Harlan Sexton, CUNY Queensborough Community College, NY; Kathy Sherak, San Francisco State University, CA; German Silva, Miami Dade College, FL; Ray Smith, Maryland English Institute, University of Maryland, MD; Shira Smith, NICE Program University of Hawaii, HI; Tara Smith, Felician College, NJ; Monica Snow, California State University, Fullerton, CA; Elaine Soffer, Nassau County Community College, NY; Andrea Spector, Santa Monica Community College, CA; Jacqueline Sport, LBWCC Luverne Center, AL; Karen Stanely, Central Piedmont Community College, NC; Susan Stern, Irvine Valley College, CA; Ayse Stromsdorfer, Soldan I.S.H.S., MO; Yilin Sun, South Seattle Community College, WA; Thomas Swietlik, Intrax International Institute, IL; Nicholas Taggert, University of Dayton, OH; Judith Tanka, UCLA Extension–American Language Center, CA; Amy Taylor, The University of Alabama Tuscaloosa, AL; Andrea Taylor, San Francisco State, CA; Priscilla Taylor, University of Southern California, CA; Ilene Teixeira, Fairfax County Public Schools, VA; Shirl H. Terrell, Collin College, TX; Marya Teutsch-Dwyer, St. Cloud State University, MN; Stephen Thergesen, ELS Language Centers, CO; Christine Tierney, Houston Community College, TX; Arlene Turini, North Moore High School, NC; Cara Tuzzolino, Nassau County Community College, NY; Suzanne Van Der Valk, Iowa State University, IA; Nathan D. Vasarhely, Ygnacio Valley High School, CA; Naomi S. Verratti, Howard Community College, MD; Hollyahna Vettori, Santa Rosa Junior College, CA; Julie Vorholt, Lewis & Clark College, OR; Danielle Wagner, FLS International Marymount College, CA; Lynn Walker, Coastline College, CA; Laura Walsh, City College of San Francisco, CA; Andrew J. Watson, The English Bakery; Donald Weasenforth, Collin College, TX; Juliane Widner, Sheepshead Bay High School, NY; Lynne Wilkins, Mills College, CA; Pamela Williams, Ventura College, CA; Jeff Wilson, Irvine Valley College, CA; James Wilson, Consomnes River College, CA; Katie Windahl, Cuyahoga Community College, OH; Dolores "Lorrie" Winter, California State University at Fullerton, CA; Jody Yamamoto, Kapi'olani Community College, HI; Ellen L. Yaniv, Boston University, MA; Norman Yoshida, Lewis & Clark College, OR; Joanna Zadra, American River College, CA; Florence Zysman, Santiago Canyon College, CA;

CANADA Patricia Birch, Brandon University, MB; Jolanta Caputa, College of New Caledonia, BC; Katherine Coburn, UBC's ELI, BC; Erin Harris-Macleod, St. Mary's University, NS; Tami Moffatt, English Language Institute, BC; Jim Papple, Brock University, ON; Robin Peace, Confederation College, BC;

ASIA Rabiatu Abubakar, Eton Language Centre, Malaysia; Wiwik Andreani, Bina Nusantara University, Indonesia; Frank Bailey, Baiko Gakuin University, Japan; Mike Baker, Kosei Junior High School, Japan; Leonard Barrow, Kanto Junior College, Japan; Herman Bartelen, Japan; Siren Betty, Fooyin University, Kaohsiung; Thomas E. Bieri, Nagoya College, Japan; Natalie Brezden, Global English House, Japan; MK Brooks, Mukogawa Women's University, Japan; Truong Ngoc Buu, The Youth Language School, Vietnam; Charles Cabell, Toyo University, Japan; Fred Carruth, Matsumoto University, Japan; Frances Causer, Seijo University, Japan; Jeffrey Chalk, SNU, South Korea; Deborah Chang, Wenzao Ursuline College of Languages, Kaohsiung; David Chatham, Ritsumeikan University, Japan; Andrew Chih Hong Chen, National Sun Yat-sen University, Kaohsiung; Christina Chen, Yu-Tsai Bilingual Elementary School, Taipei; Hui-chen Chen, Shi-Lin High School of Commerce, Taipei; Seungmoon Choe, K2M Language Institute, South Korea; Jason Jeffree Cole, Coto College, Japan; Le Minh Cong, Vungtau Tourism Vocational College, Vietnam; Todd Cooper, Toyama National College of Technology, Japan; Marie Cosgrove, Daito Bunka University, Japan; Randall Cotten, Gifu City Women's College, Japan; Tony Cripps, Ritsumeikan University, Japan; Andy Cubalit, CHS, Thailand; Daniel Cussen, Takushoku University, Japan; Le Dan, Ho Chi Minh City Electric Power College, Vietnam; Simon Daykin, Banghwa-dong Community Centre, South Korea; Aimee Denham, ILA, Vietnam; Bryan Dickson, David's English Center, Taipei; Nathan Ducker, Japan University, Japan; Ian Duncan, Simul International Corporate Training, Japan; Nguyen Thi Kieu Dung, Thang Long University, Vietnam; Truong Quang Dung, Tien Giang University, Vietnam; Nguyen Thi Thuy Duong, Vietnamese American Vocational Training College, Vietnam; Wong Tuck Ee, Raja Tun Azlan Science Secondary School, Malaysia; Emilia Effendy, International Islamic University Malaysia, Malaysia; Bettizza Escueta, KMUTT, Thailand; Robert Eva, Kaisei Girls High School, Japan; Jim George, Luna International Language School, Japan; Jurgen Germeys, Silk Road Language Center, South Korea; Wong Ai Gnoh, SMJK Chung Hwa Confucian, Malaysia; Sarah Go, Seoul Women's University, South Korea; Peter Goosselink, Hokkai High School, Japan; Robert Gorden, SNU, South Korea; Wendy M. Gough, St. Mary College/Nunoike Gaigo Senmon Gakko, Japan; Tim Grose, Sapporo Gakuin University, Japan; Pham Thu Ha, Le Van Tam Primary School, Vietnam; Ann-Marie Hadzima, Taipei; Troy Hammond, Tokyo Gakugei University International Secondary School, Japan; Robiatul 'Adawiah Binti Hamzah, SMK Putrajaya Precinct 8(1), Malaysia; Tran Thi Thuy Hang, Ho Chi Minh City Banking University, Vietnam; To Thi Hong Hanh, CEFALT, Vietnam; George Hays, Tokyo Kokusai Daigaku, Japan; Janis Hearn, Hongik University, South Korea; Chantel Hemmi, Jochi Daigaku, Japan; David Hindman, Sejong University, South Korea; Nahn Cam Hoa, Ho Chi Minh City University of Technology, Vietnam; Jana Holt, Korea University, South Korea; Jason Hollowell, Nihon University, Japan; F. N. (Zoe) Hsu, National Tainan University, Yong Kang; Kuei-ping Hsu, National Tsing Hua University, Hsinchu City; Wenhua Hsu, I-Shou University, Kaohsiung; Luu Nguyen Quoc Hung, Cantho University, Vietnam; Cecile Hwang, Changwon National University, South Korea; Ainol Haryati Ibrahim, Universiti Malaysia Pahang, Malaysia; Robert Jeens, Yonsei University, South Korea; Linda M. Joyce, Kyushu Sangyo University, Japan; Dr. Nisai Kaewsanchai, English Square Kanchanaburi, Thailand; Aniza Kamarulzaman, Sabah Science Secondary School, Malaysia; Ikuko Kashiwabara, Osaka Electro-Communication University, Japan; Gurmit Kaur, INTI College, Malaysia; Nick Keane, Japan; Ward Ketcheson, Aomori University, Japan; Nicholas Kemp, Kyushu International University, Japan; Montchatry Ketmuni, Rajamangala University of Technology, Thailand; Dinh Viet Khanh, Vietnam; Seonok Kim, Kangsu Jongro Language School, South Korea; Suyeon Kim, Anyang University, South Korea; Kelly P. Kimura, Soka University, Japan; Masakazu Kimura, Katoh Gakuen Gyoshu High School, Japan; Gregory King, Chubu Daigaku, Japan; Stan Kirk, Konan University, Japan; Donald Knight, Nan Hua/Fu Li Junior High Schools, Hsinchu; Kari J. Kostiainen, Nagoya City University, Japan; Pattri Kuanpulpol, Silpakorn University, Thailand; Ha Thi Lan, Thai Binh Teacher Training College, Vietnam; Eric Edwin Larson, Miyazaki Prefectural Nursing University, Japan; David Laurence, Chubu Daigaku, Japan; Richard S. Lavin, Prefectural University of Kumamoto, Japan; Shirley Leane, Chugoku Junior College, Japan; I-Hsiu Lee, Yunlin; Nari Lee, Park Jung PLS, South Korea; Tae Lee, Yonsei University, South Korea; Lys Yongsoon Lee, Reading Town Geumcheon, South Korea; Mallory Leece, Sun Moon University, South Korea; Dang Hong Lien, Tan Lam Upper Secondary School, Vietnam; Huang Li-Han, Rebecca Education Institute, Taipei; Sovannarith Lim, Royal University of Phnom Penh, Cambodia; Ginger Lin, National Kaohsiung Hospitality College, Kaohsiung; Noel Lineker, New Zealand/Japan; Tran Dang Khanh Linh, Nha Trang Teachers' Training College, Vietnam; Daphne Liu, Buliton English School, Taipei; S. F. Josephine Liu, Tien-Mu Elementary School, Taipei ; Caroline Luo, Tunghai University, Taichung; Jeng-Jia Luo, Tunghai University, Taichung; Laura MacGregor, Gakushuin University, Japan; Amir Madani, Visuttharangsi School, Thailand; Elena Maeda, Sacred Heart Professional Training College, Japan; Vu Thi Thanh Mai, Hoang Gia Education Center, Vietnam; Kimura Masakazu, Kato Gakuen Gyoshu High School, Japan; Susumu Matsuhashi, Net Link English School, Japan; James McCrostie, Daito Bunka University, Japan; Joel McKee, Inha University, South Korea; Colin McKenzie, Wachirawit Primary School, Thailand; Terumi Miyazoe, Tokyo Denki Daigaku, Japan; William K. Moore, Hiroshima Kokusai Gakuin University, Japan; Kevin Mueller, Tokyo Kokusai Daigaku, Japan; Hudson Murrell, Baiko Gakuin University, Japan; Frances Namba, Senri International School of Kwansei Gakuin, Japan; Keiichi Narita, Niigata University, Japan; Kim Chung Nguyen, Ho Chi Minh University of

Industry, Vietnam; **Do Thi Thanh Nhan**, Hanoi University, Vietnam; **Dale Kazuo Nishi**, Aoyama English Conversation School, Japan; **Huynh Thi Ai Nguyen**, Vietnam; **Dongshin Oh**, YBM PLS, South Korea; **Keiko Okada**, Dokkyo Daigaku, Japan; **Louise Ohashi**, Shukutoku University, Japan; **Yongjun Park**, Sangji University, South Korea; **Donald Patnaude**, Ajarn Donald's English Language Services, Thailand; **Virginia Peng**, Ritsumeikan University, Japan; **Suangkanok Piboonthamnont**, Rajamangala University of Technology, Thailand; **Simon Pitcher**, Business English Teaching Services, Japan; **John C. Probert**, New Education Worldwide, Thailand; **Do Thi Hoa Quyen**, Ton Duc Thang University, Vietnam; **John P. Racine**, Dokkyo University, Japan; **Kevin Ramsden**, Kyoto University of Foreign Studies, Japan; **Luis Rappaport**, Cung Thieu Nha Ha Noi, Vietnam; **Lisa Reshad**, Konan Daigaku Hyogo, Japan; **Peter Riley**, Taisho University, Japan; **Thomas N. Robb**, Kyoto Sangyo University, Japan; **Rory Rosszell**, Meiji Daigaku, Japan; **Maria Feti Rosyani**, Universitas Kristen Indonesia, Indonesia; **Greg Rouault**, Konan University, Japan; **Chris Ruddenklau**, Kindai University, Japan; **Hans-Gustav Schwartz**, Thailand; **Mary-Jane Scott**, Soongsil University, South Korea; **Dara Sheahan**, Seoul National University, South Korea; **James Sherlock**, A.P.W. Angthong, Thailand; **Prof. Shieh**, Minghsin University of Science & Technology, Xinfeng; **Yuko Shimizu**, Ritsumeikan University, Japan; **Suzila Mohd Shukor**, Universiti Sains Malaysia, Malaysia; **Stephen E. Smith**, Mahidol University, Thailand; **Moon-young Son**, South Korea; **Seunghee Son**, Anyang University, South Korea; **Mi-young Song**, Kyungwon University, South Korea; **Lisa Sood**, VUS, BIS, Vietnam; **Jason Stewart**, Taejon International Language School, South Korea; **Brian A. Stokes**, Korea University, South Korea; **Mulder Su**, Shih-Chien University, Kaohsiung; **Yoomi Suh**, English Plus, South Korea; **Yun-Fang Sun**, Wenzao Ursuline College of Languages, Kaohsiung; **Richard Swingle**, Kansai Gaidai University, Japan; **Sanford Taborn**, Kinjo Gakuin Daigaku, Japan; **Mamoru Takahashi**, Akita Prefectural University, Japan; **Tran Hoang Tan**, School of International Training, Vietnam; **Takako Tanaka**, Doshisha University, Japan; **Jeffrey Taschner**, American University Alumni Language Center, Thailand; **Matthew Taylor**, Kinjo Gakuin Daigaku, Japan; **Michael Taylor**, International Pioneers School, Thailand; **Kampanart Thammaphati**, Wattana Wittaya Academy, Thailand; **Tran Duong The**, Sao Mai Language Center, Vietnam; **Tran Dinh Tho**, Duc Tri Secondary School, Vietnam; **Huynh Thi Anh Thu**, Nhatrang College of Culture Arts and Tourism, Vietnam; **Peter Timmins**, Peter's English School, Japan; **Fumie Togano**, Hosei Daini High School, Japan; **F. Sigmund Topor**, Keio University Language School, Japan; **Tu Trieu**, Rise VN, Vietnam; **Yen-Cheng Tseng**, Chang-Jung Christian University, Tainan; **Pei-Hsuan Tu**, National Cheng Kung University, Tainan City; **Hajime Uematsu**, Hirosaki University, Japan; **Rachel Um**, Mok-dong Oedae English School, South Korea; **David Underhill**, EEExpress, Japan; **Ben Underwood**, Kugenuma High School, Japan; **Siriluck Usaha**, Sripatum University, Thailand; **Tyas Budi Utami**, Indonesia; **Nguyen Thi Van**, Far East International School, Vietnam; **Stephan Van Eycken**, Kosei Gakuen Girls High School, Japan; **Zisa Velasquez**, Taihu International School/Semarang International School, China/Indonesia; **Jeffery Walter**, Sangji University, South Korea; **Bill White**, Kinki University, Japan; **Yohanes De Deo Widyastoko**, Xaverius Senior High School, Indonesia; **Dylan Williams**, SNU, South Korea; **Jisuk Woo**, Ichean University, South Korea; **Greg Chung-Hsien Wu**, Providence University, Taichung; **Xun Xiaoming**, BLCU, China; **Hui-Lien Yeh**, Chai Nan University of Pharmacy and Science, Tainan; **Sittiporn Yodnil**, Huachiew Chalermprakiet University, Thailand; **Shamshul Helmy Zambahari**, Universiti Teknologi Malaysia, Malaysia; **Ming-Yuli**, Chang Jung Christian University, Tainan; **Aimin Fadhlee bin Mahmud Zuhodi**, Kuala Terengganu Science School, Malaysia;

TURKEY **Shirley F. Akis**, American Culture Association/Fomara; **Gül Akkoç**, Boğaziçi University; **Seval Akmeşe**, Haliç University; **Ayşenur Akyol**, Ege University; **Ayşe Umut Aribaş**, Beykent University; **Gökhan Asan**, Kapadokya Vocational College; **Hakan Asan**, Kapadokya Vocational College; **Julia Asan**, Kapadokya Vocational College; **Azarvan Atac**, Piri Reis University; **Nur Babat**, Kapadokya Vocational College; **Feyza Balakbabalar**, Kadir Has University; **Gözde Balikçi**, Beykent University; **Deniz Balım**, Haliç University; **Asli Başdoğan**, Kadir Has University; **Ayla Bayram**, Kapadokya Vocational College; **Pinar Bilgiç**, Kadir Has University; **Kenan Bozkurt**, Kapadokya Vocational College; **Yonca Bozkurt**, Ege University; **Frank Carr**, Piri Reis; **Mengü Noyan Çengel**, Ege University; **Elif Doğan**, Ege University; **Natalia Donmez**, 29 Mayis Üniverste; **Nalan Emirsoy**, Kadir Has University; **Ayşe Engin**, Kadir Has University; **Ayhan Gedikbaş**, Ege University; **Gülşah Gençer**, Beykent University; **Seyit Ömer Gök**, Gediz University; **Tuğba Gök**, Gediz University; **İlkay Gökçe**, Ege University; **Zeynep Birinci Guler**, Maltepe University; **Neslihan Güler**, Kadir Has University; **Sircan Gümüş**, Kadir Has University; **Nesrin Gündoğu**, T.C. Piri Reis University; **Tanju Gurpinar**, Piri Reis University; **Selin Gurturk**, Piri Reis University; **Neslihan Gurutku**, Piri Reis University; **Roger Hewitt**, Maltepe University; **Nilüfer İbrahimoğlu**, Beykent University; **Nevin Kaftelen**, Kadir Has University; **Sultan Kalin**, Kapadokya Vocational College; **Sema Kaplan Karabina**, Anadolu University; **Eray Kara**, Giresun University; **Beylü Karayazgan**, Ege University; **Darren Kelso**, Piri Reis University; **Trudy Kittle**, Kapadokya Vocational College; **Şaziye Konaç**, Kadir Has University; **Güneş Korkmaz**, Kapadokya Vocational College; **Robert Ledbury**, Izmir University of Economics; **Ashley Lucas**, Maltepe University; **Bülent Nedium Uça**, Dogus University; **Murat Nurlu**, Ege University; **Mollie Owens**, Kadir Has University; **Oya Özağaç**, Boğaziçi University; **Funda Özcan**, Ege University; **İlkay Özdemir**, Ege University; **Ülkü Öztürk**, Gediz University; **Cassondra Puls**, Anadolu University; **Yelda Sarikaya**, Cappadocia Vocational College; **Müge Şekercioğlu**, Ege University; **Melis Senol**, Canakkale Onsekiz Mart University, The School of Foreign Languages; **Patricia Sümer**, Kadir Has University; **Rex Surface**, Beykent University; **Mustafa Torun**, Kapadokya Vocational College; **Tansel Üstünloğlu**, Ege University; **Fatih Yücel**, Beykent University; **Şule Yüksel**, Ege University;

THE MIDDLE EAST **Amina Saif Mohammed Al Hashamia**, Nizwa College of Applied Sciences, Oman; **Jennifer Baran**, Kuwait University, Kuwait; **Phillip Chappells**, GEMS Modern Academy, U.A.E.; **Sharon Ruth Devaneson**, Ibri College of Technology, Oman; **Hanaa El-Deeb**, Canadian International College, Egypt; **Yvonne Eaton**, Community College of Qatar, Qatar; **Brian Gay**, Sultan Qaboos University, Oman; **Gail Al Hafidh**, Sharjah Women's College (HCT), U.A.E.; **Jonathan Hastings**, American Language Center, Jordan; **Laurie Susan Hilu**, English Language Centre, University of Bahrain, Bahrain; **Abraham Irannezhad**, Mehre Aval, Iran; **Kevin Kempe**, CNA-Q, Qatar; **Jill Newby James**, University of Nizwa; **Mary Kay Klein**, American University of Sharjah, U.A.E.; **Sian Khoury**, Fujairah Women's College (HCT), U.A.E.; **Hussein Dehghan Manshadi**, Farhang Pajooh & Jaam-e-Jam Language School, Iran; **Jessica March**, American University of Sharjah, U.A.E.; **Neil McBeath**, Sultan Qaboos University, Oman; **Sandy McDonagh**, Abu Dhabi Men's College (HCT), U.A.E.; **Rob Miles**, Sharjah Women's College (HCT), U.A.E.; **Michael Kevin Neumann**, Al Ain Men's College (HCT), U.A.E.;

LATIN AMERICA **Aldana Aguirre**, Argentina; **Claudia Almeida**, Coordenação de Idiomas, Brazil; **Cláudia Arias**, Brazil; **Maria de los Angeles Barba**, FES Acatlan UNAM, Mexico; **Lilia Barrios**, Universidad Autónoma de Tamaulipas, Mexico; **Adán Beristain**, UAEM, Mexico; **Ricardo Böck**, Manoel Ribas, Brazil; **Edson Braga**, CNA, Brazil; **Marli Buttelli**, Mater et Magistra, Brazil; **Alessandra Campos**, Inova Centro de Linguas, Brazil; **Priscila Catta Preta Ribeiro**, Brazil; **Gustavo Cestari**, Access International School, Brazil; **Walter D'Alessandro**, Virginia Language Center, Brazil; **Lilian De Gennaro**, Argentina; **Mônica De Stefani**, Quality Centro de Idiomas, Brazil; **Julio Alejandro Flores**, BUAP, Mexico; **Mirian Freire**, CNA Vila Guilherme, Brazil; **Francisco Garcia**, Colegio Lestonnac de San Angel, Mexico; **Miriam Giovanardi**, Brazil; **Darlene Gonzalez Miy**, ITESM CCV, Mexico; **Maria Laura Grimaldi**, Argentina; **Luz Dary Guzmán**, IMPAHU, Colombia; **Carmen Koppe**, Brazil; **Monica Krutzler**, Brazil; **Marcus Murilo Lacerda**, Seven Idiomas, Brazil; **Nancy Lake**, CEL-LEP, Brazil; **Cris Lazzerini**, Brazil; **Sandra Luna**, Argentina; **Ricardo Luvisan**, Brazil; **Jorge Murilo Menezes**, ACBEU, Brazil; **Monica Navarro**, Instituto Cultural A. C., Mexico; **Joacyr Oliveira**, Faculdades Metropolitanas Unidas and Summit School for Teachers, Brazil; **Ayrton Cesar Oliveira de Araujo**, E&A English Classes, Brazil; **Ana Laura Oriente**, Seven Idiomas, Brazil; **Adelia Peña Clavel**, CELE UNAM, Mexico; **Beatriz Pereira**, Summit School, Brazil; **Miguel Perez**, Instituto Cultural, Mexico; **Cristiane Perone**, Associação Cultura Inglesa, Brazil; **Pamela Claudia Pogré**, Colegio Integral Caballito / Universidad de Flores, Argentina; **Dalva Prates**, Brazil; **Marianne Rampaso**, Iowa Idiomas, Brazil; **Daniela Rutolo**, Instituto Superior Cultural Británico, Argentina; **Maione Sampaio**, Maione Carrijo Consultoria em Inglês Ltda, Brazil; **Elaine Santesso**, TS Escola de Idiomas, Brazil; **Camila Francisco Santos**, UNS Idiomas, Brazil; **Lucia Silva**, Cooplem Idiomas, Brazil; **Maria Adela Sorzio**, Instituto Superior Santa Cecilia, Argentina; **Elcio Souza**, Unibero, Brazil; **Willie Thomas**, Rainbow Idiomas, Brazil; **Sandra Villegas**, Instituto Humberto de Paolis, Argentina; **John Whelan**, La Universidad Nacional Autonoma de Mexico, Mexico

CONTENTS

READING	▶	identifying main ideas and supporting details
VOCABULARY	▶	using the dictionary to identify word forms
WRITING	▶	organizing and developing a paragraph
GRAMMAR	▶	real conditionals: present and future

Q?

UNIT QUESTION

How do you make a good first impression?

A Discuss these questions with your classmates.

1. What qualities do you look for in a friend?

2. What is the best way to make a good first impression on a classmate? On a boss?

3. Look at the photo. Describe the people in the room. Where are they? What is the woman doing?

UNIT
OBJECTIVE ▶▶▶▶ Read the articles and gather information and ideas to write a paragraph on how to make a good first impression.

B Listen to *The Q Classroom* online. Then match the suggestions in the box with the students.

a. be polite	b. comb my hair	c. have confidence	d. keep eye contact
e. pay attention	f. remember people's names	g. smile	h. wear nice clothes

How do you make a good first impression?	
Marcus	b. comb my hair, h. wear nice clothes
Yuna	
Felix	
Sophy	

C Go to the Online Discussion Board to discuss the Unit Question with your classmates.

D Look at the questionnaire. Choose the answer that makes each statement true for you.

Do You Make a Good First Impression?

1. **When I talk to someone I don't know, …**
   - ○ a. I feel uncomfortable.
   - ○ b. I can usually find something to talk about.
   - ○ c. I ask a lot of questions.

2. **When I go to a restaurant, I usually wear…**
   - ○ a. casual clothes like jeans, a t-shirt, and sneakers.
   - ○ b. nice clothes, but nothing too professional.
   - ○ c. very professional clothes.

3. **When I am sitting, I usually…**
   - ○ a. sit up straight.
   - ○ b. do not sit up straight.
   - ○ c. take up a lot of space.

4. **When I need to get someone's attention, I…**
   - ○ a. speak loudly or shout.
   - ○ b. say, "Excuse me" first.
   - ○ c. tap the person on the arm or shoulder.

5. **My friends and family talk to me about my manners…**
   - ○ a. often.
   - ○ b. sometimes.
   - ○ c. never.

6. **I usually speak…**
   - ○ a. a little more formally than most people.
   - ○ b. about the same as other people.
   - ○ c. less formally than other people.

7. **When I meet someone for the first time, …**
   - ○ a. I do most of the talking.
   - ○ b. I talk about half the time and listen half the time.
   - ○ c. I listen and let the other person talk.

8. **When people first meet me, they often think I am…**
   - ○ a. very serious.
   - ○ b. shy and a little nervous.
   - ○ c. outgoing and friendly.
   - ○ d. other _____.

E Look at your answers above. Do you think you make a good first impression? Discuss your answers with a partner.

READING 1 | Small Talk: A Big Deal

UNIT OBJECTIVE ▶▶▶▶ You are going to read an online newspaper article about small talk. Use the article to gather information and ideas for your Unit Assignment.

PREVIEW THE READING

A. PREVIEW Read the title and headings and look at the photographs. What do you think "small talk" means? Check (✓) your answer.

☐ talking about important events in your life

☐ talking about things like traffic or weather

☐ talking about your boss and coworkers

Writing **Tip**

When you quick-write, try to keep writing without stopping. Focus on your ideas.

B. QUICK WRITE How do you feel when you meet someone new at school or at work? What do you say to make him or her feel more comfortable? Write for 5–10 minutes in response. Be sure to use this section for your Unit Assignment.

C. VOCABULARY Check (✓) the words you know. Then work with a partner to locate each word in the reading. Use clues to help define the words you don't know. Check your definitions in the dictionary.

appreciate *(v.)* 🔑	lead to *(phr. v.)* 🔑
confidence *(n.)* 🔑	maintain *(v.)* 🔑
demonstrate *(v.)* 🔑	offensive *(adj.)* 🔑
effective *(adj.)* 🔑	select *(v.)* 🔑
impress *(v.)* 🔑	stranger *(n.)* 🔑

🔑 Oxford 3000™ words

 D. Go online to listen and practice your pronunciation.

🔊 **A.** Read the article and gather information about how to make a good first impression.

Small Talk: A Big Deal

1   Put a group of **strangers** in a room together, and they'll probably start a conversation. "Hot today, isn't it?" one might say. "You said it," another replies. Soon enough, comments about today's weather will **lead to** other people's weather stories about getting stuck in the rain or trying to stay cool during last week's high of 100 degrees Fahrenheit (37.7 degrees Celsius).

2   Why do we talk so much about the weather, and why is it important? When we first meet people, we don't begin by telling them our life story. We start with *small talk*, a polite conversation about something much less important like traffic or weather. Sometimes it goes nowhere. We may talk to people in the elevator, at the store, or on the bus, but the conversation quickly ends. Many other times, however, small talk can create something *much* bigger, including new friendships or even a better job. It just has to be done the right way.

New Friends and Jobs

3   Research suggests that small talk can build new friendships. When we begin conversations with new people, we want to feel comfortable, and so do they. We use small talk to find common interests. Weather may lead to more interesting topics like summer fashion or winter foods. Once we have a common interest, a friendship can begin. The more we engage in[1] small talk, the more friends we can make.

4   Small talk even helps people get hired and perform better at work. In order to **impress** at a job interview, you need to bond with the interviewer right away. **Effective** small talk can make that first impression get you the job. Small talk is equally important after you are hired. In fact, research

[1] **engage in:** to take part in something

demonstrates that just five minutes of small talk can lead to more successful business deals. Effective small talk at the office can also help people get promoted[2] more often.

As Easy as 1-2-3

5 So, how can you make small talk lead to a new friendship, job, or promotion? First off, find common ground. **Select** something around you that you share with the other person. At a job interview, look around the room for common interests. Perhaps the interviewer has a photo of his children on his desk. "Oh, you have kids, too?" you might ask.

6 Next, keep the conversation going. Compliment[3] the other person to make him or her feel comfortable, and ask questions to show interest: "Oh, you've been to Paris?" Don't do all the talking, and avoid saying anything **offensive** that might make the other person feel awkward. It could create a negative impression and possibly end the conversation.

7 Third, **maintain** eye contact. When you look people in the eye, they feel you **appreciate** what they are saying. Maintaining eye contact is important. It makes you appear honest and builds trust. Without trust, a relationship cannot develop[4], say experts.

The Big Question: To Talk or Not to Talk?

8 Some people shy away from small talk. They might not have enough **confidence** to start up conversations with strangers. And let's face it—talking to someone you don't know is not the easiest thing to do! Still, experts say with practice, small talk *does* get easier, even for the shy ones. You just have to take that first step.

9 Other people avoid small talk because they dislike discussing things like traffic, weather, or sports scores. For them, these topics are just *too* small. However, when you think about it, small talk is anything but small. In fact, it is actually a *very* big deal!

---

[2] **promote:** to move someone to a higher rank or more senior job

[3] **compliment:** to praise or express admiration for someone

[4] **develop:** to become better and stronger

Vocabulary
Skill Review

Look at the sentences
in Activity B. Which of
the vocabulary words
in bold are nouns?
Which are verbs?

B. VOCABULARY **Here are some words from Reading 1. Read the sentences. Then match each bold word with its definition below.**

_f_   1. I thought I saw a **stranger** standing in front of my apartment building, but then I realized it was my friend waiting for me.

____ 2. Smiling can **demonstrate** to other people that you are a friendly person. Shaking a person's hand is another way to show friendliness.

____ 3. People with **confidence** usually make better public speakers because they feel very comfortable standing in front of a lot of people.

____ 4. Many people believe Facebook is an **effective** way to keep in touch with family and friends who live far away.

____ 5. When you meet new people in school, it can sometimes **lead to** friendships that last a lifetime.

____ 6. You should **select** what you wear to a job interview carefully. What you wear to an interview is very important.

____ 7. I really **appreciate** my friends. They always give me good advice.

____ 8. Adel wanted to **impress** the interviewer, so he told him about the important project he worked on.

____ 9. One of the best ways to **maintain** a conversation is to keep asking questions; then it can easily continue.

____ 10. Jokes are a great way to "break the ice" when you meet new people, but you should never tell **offensive** jokes that could make them feel uncomfortable or angry.

a. (*phr. v.*) to have something as a result

b. (*n.*) the feeling that you are sure about your own beliefs or abilities

c. (*v.*) to make someone admire and respect you

d. (*adj.*) producing the result that is wanted or intended

e. (*v.*) to choose someone or something from similar people or things

f. (*n.*) a person you do not know

g. (*v.*) to enjoy or to understand the value of someone or something

h. (*adj.*) unpleasant or insulting

i. (*v.*) to show or explain how to do something

j. (*v.*) to continue to have something; to keep something at the same level

 C. Go online for more practice with the vocabulary.

D. Circle the main idea of the article.

a. Strangers who find themselves together in the same place will probably talk to each other.

b. Small talk is a polite conversation with strangers about topics like traffic, weather, or sports.

c. According to experts, there are three important steps to follow when you engage in small talk.

d. When small talk is done correctly, it can improve people's social and professional lives.

E. Read the statements. Write *T* (true) or *F* (false). Then correct each false statement to make it true according to the article.

____ 1. People do not usually talk about their personal lives with strangers.

____ 2. Small talk can happen at the store or on the bus.

____ 3. Small talk helps people find shared interests.

____ 4. Small talk is only helpful before you get a job.

____ 5. Just five minutes of small talk helps employees get promoted.

____ 6. You should never ask new people details about their family.

____ 7. Some people feel uncomfortable using small talk.

____ 8. Effective small talk can leave a bad first impression on others.

 **Tip for Success**

Use pronoun referents, such as *it* and *they*, to continue an idea in a following sentence.

F. Read these sentences from Reading 1. Then answer the questions. Find the sentences in the reading to help you.

1. (Paragraph 1) Put a group of strangers in a room together, and **they**'ll probably start a conversation.

   Who does ***they*** refer to? _____

2. (Paragraph 2) **It** just has to be done the right way.

   What does ***it*** refer to? _____

3. (Paragraph 3) When we begin conversations with new people, we want to feel comfortable, and so do **they**.

   Who does ***they*** refer to? _____

4. (Paragraph 6) **It** could create a negative impression and possibly end the conversation.

   What does ***it*** refer to? _____

5. (Paragraph 7) **It** makes you appear honest and builds trust.

   What does *it* refer to? _____

6. (Paragraph 8) **They** might not have enough confidence to start up conversations with strangers.

   Who does *they* refer to? _____

Critical Thinking

Activity G asks you to identify a **causal chain**. A causal chain is a series of causes and effects. When you organize ideas into a causal chain, it will help you to see how one event affects another event, which then affects another event.

G. Read paragraph 3 of Reading 1 and complete this graphic organizer. Identify the causal chain in the paragraph. Write the correct answers in the boxes.

a. We find common interests.

b. ~~We begin a conversation with a stranger.~~

c. A new friendship starts.

d. We discuss more interesting topics.

e. We use small talk.

H. The author suggests that there is also a *wrong* way to use small talk. What do you think the wrong way might be? Write 5–8 sentences giving your opinion. Then share your paragraph with a partner and compare your ideas.

I. Go online to read *Professional Email Etiquette* and check your comprehension.

WRITE WHAT YOU THINK

A. Discuss these questions in a group.

1. When was the last time you used small talk? Describe the situation.

2. Do you agree with the author that small talk is "a big deal"? Why or why not?

B. Choose one question and write a paragraph in response. Look back at your Quick Write on page 5 as you think about what you learned.

A paragraph is a group of sentences about the same topic. The **main idea** is usually given in the first sentence. This is called the **topic sentence**. Sometimes the topic sentence can also be the last sentence or in the middle of a paragraph. The other sentences are called supporting sentences and contain **supporting details**, such as examples, explanations, facts, definitions, and reasons.

Identifying main ideas and supporting details is an important skill that will help you become a more effective reader. When you read, skim for main ideas and scan for details.

A. Read the sentences from Reading 1. Write *MI* for the main idea of the paragraph. Write *SD* for the supporting details.

1. Paragraph 3

   ____ **a.** Weather may lead to more interesting topics like summer fashion or winter foods.

   ____ **b.** Research suggests that small talk can build new friendships.

   ____ **c.** The more we engage in small talk, the more friends we can make.

2. Paragraph 4

   ____ **a.** In order to impress at a job interview, you need to bond with the interviewer right away.

   ____ **b.** In fact, research demonstrates that just five minutes of small talk can lead to more successful business deals.

   ____ **c.** Small talk even helps people get hired and perform better at work.

3. Paragraph 5

   ____ **a.** So, how can you make small talk lead to a new friendship, job, or promotion?

   ____ **b.** First off, find common ground.

   ____ **c.** At a job interview, look around the room for common interests.

B. Look again at paragraphs 1, 6, 7, and 8 in Reading 1. Underline the topic sentence that states each paragraph's main idea. Then compare your answers with a partner.

 **C.** Go online for more practice identifying main ideas and supporting details.

UNIT OBJECTIVE ▶▶▶▶ You are going to read an article from a career magazine about job interviews. Use the article to gather information and ideas for your Unit Assignment.

PREVIEW THE READING

A. **PREVIEW** Read the title and first sentence of each paragraph. Check (✓) all the things you think the article will say you should do at a job interview.

☐ Find out as much as you can about the job.

☐ Wear your most comfortable clothing.

☐ Don't smile; you want the interviewer to take you seriously.

☐ Let the interviewer do all the talking.

☐ Don't interrupt the interviewer when he or she is talking.

B. **QUICK WRITE** What advice would you give to someone on a job interview? What should he or she do and not do? Write for 5–10 minutes in response. Be sure to use this section for your Unit Assignment.

C. **VOCABULARY** Check (✓) the words you know. Use a dictionary to define any new or unknown words. Then discuss how the words will relate to the unit with a partner.

accomplishment *(n.)*	**punctual** *(adj.)*
consider *(v.)* 🔑	**research** *(n.)* 🔑
exaggerate *(v.)* 🔑	**responsible** *(adj.)* 🔑
expect *(v.)* 🔑	**slang** *(n.)*
professional *(adj.)* 🔑	**weakness** *(n.)* 🔑

🔑 Oxford 3000™ words

 D. Go online to listen and practice your pronunciation.

WORK WITH THE READING

A. Read the article and gather information about how to make a good first impression.

Job Interviews 101

1 You finally got that call you have been waiting for—an interview for a new job. At first, you will probably feel overjoyed[1], but as the interview gets closer, you are likely to get more and more nervous about the big day. Experts say that you only have 30 seconds to make a good first impression at a job interview. The key to a successful interview is to be prepared and stay **professional** at all times. To make sure you do your best, remember these ten tips:

2 *Be prepared.* Learn as much as you can about the company before the interview. Go to the business's website and read it so you are aware of how things work there. Think of questions the interviewer might ask you and practice your answers with a friend. Know how to discuss both your strengths and your **weaknesses** because you will be asked about both!

3 *Dress the part.* If you walk in wearing jeans and a T-shirt, you are not likely to get the position. Wear clothing that is neat, clean, and presentable. Most companies **expect** applicants to wear business clothes, such as a shirt and tie or a nice suit. Dressing well shows that you are serious about the job.

4 *Be **punctual**.* Arriving late to an interview can be deadly. No employer wants to hire someone who is not **responsible** enough to come to work on time. Get to the interview 10–15 minutes early to help yourself relax before you step into the office.

5 *Make eye contact.* Look your interviewer in the eye when you greet him or her and keep eye contact throughout the entire interview. Keeping eye contact shows the other person that you are both honest and confident.

6 *Be polite.* Sit up straight when you are being interviewed, listen carefully to what the interviewer is saying, and avoid using **slang** or bad words. If you don't understand a question, ask politely, "Could you please repeat that?" When you are polite, you appear more professional and are more likely to get the job.

7 *Don't interrupt[2].* Interrupting is **considered** rude. Let the interviewer finish what she or he is saying. If you have something important to say, try to remember it and wait for a moment of silence to speak up.

8 *Find shared interests.* Try to notice what the interviewer finds important. Listen for

---

[1] **overjoyed:** very happy   [2] **interrupt:** to make somebody stop speaking

topics that you both know something about and discuss them. If you can't think of anything, nod[3] yes or agree with points that the interviewer makes.

9   *Sell yourself.* Don't be afraid to talk about your **accomplishments**. Employers want to hire people who are successful and confident in their abilities. However, be careful not to **exaggerate**. Do not lie about past job responsibilities. You don't want employers to ask your old boss about things you never did!

10   *Stay positive.* Avoid complaining about a bad boss or job you had before. Being negative can make employers worry that you are not a team player, or that you don't work well with others. And remember to smile. Smiling shows you are easygoing and enthusiastic.

11   *Ask questions.* At the end of the interview, ask specific questions about the job or company, such as "What kind of work can I expect to be doing the first year?" or "Where do you see the company five years from now?" You want to show the employer that you have done your **research** and that you care about working there.

12   Interviewing is not easy, but it is easier when you know what to do and what to expect. If you stay honest and professional, you will get yourself one step closer to the job you want. Oh, and one more thing: don't forget to breathe!

---

[3] **nod:** to move your head down and then up again quickly as a way of saying yes

B. VOCABULARY **Complete each sentence with the vocabulary from Reading 2.**

accomplishment *(n.)*	professional *(adj.)*	responsible *(adj.)*
consider *(v.)*	punctual *(adj.)*	slang *(n.)*
exaggerate *(v.)*	research *(n.)*	weakness *(n.)*
expect *(v.)*		

1.   In the interview, Scott did not _____ his work experience. He knew his six months in sales wasn't a lot, but he wouldn't lie.

2.   My boss is a great person, but he has one _____. He almost never smiles, even when things are going well!

3.   You are not allowed to use your cell phone in some restaurants because many people _____ it rude.

4.   Alain is always _____. He's never late for anything.

5.   Many teenagers use so much _____ when they talk to each other that their own parents can't understand them.

6. Takeshi is very _____. He always pays his bills on time.

7. You were late for work again today. I _____ you to arrive on time tomorrow.

8. A friend told me about a good company, so I did some _____ online. I learned that it was one of the top companies to work for here.

9. When you speak to customers, you should always be _____. You should be polite and try to help them as quickly as you can.

10. Getting a job as an accountant has been my greatest professional _____. It's something I dreamed about for years.

iQ ONLINE **C.** **Go online for more practice with the vocabulary.**

D. Complete the T-chart with information from the article.

Job Interview *Dos*	Job Interview *Don'ts*
Dress professionally.	Don't be negative.

E. **Read the statements. Write *T* (true) or *F* (false). Then correct each false statement to make it true according to the article.**

____ 1. Learn as much as you can about the company before the interview.

____ 2. Most companies expect you to wear casual clothes to an interview.

____ 3. Arrive 30–40 minutes early so you can start the interview early.

____ 4. Keeping eye contact shows that you are confident.

____ 5. It's OK to lie a little about a past job to impress the interviewer.

____ 6. Avoid complaining about a boss you had before.

____ 7. At the end of the interview, tell the interviewer a personal story.

F. Match these main ideas from the reading with the correct supporting details below. Then read the article again to check your answers.

____ 1. Be prepared.   ____ 4. Be polite.   ____ 7. Sell yourself.

____ 2. Dress the part.   ____ 5. Don't interrupt.   ____ 8. Stay positive.

____ 3. Be punctual.   ____ 6. Find shared interests.

a. If you have something important to say, try to remember it and wait for a moment of silence to speak up.

b. If you don't understand a question, ask politely, "Could you please repeat that?"

c. Most companies expect applicants to wear business clothes.

d. Being negative can make employers worry that you are not a team player.

e. No employer wants to hire someone who is not responsible enough to come to work on time.

f. Think of questions the interviewer might ask you.

g. Employers want to hire people who are successful and confident.

h. Listen for topics that you both know something about and discuss them.

 WRITE WHAT YOU THINK

A. Discuss the questions in a group. Look back at your Quick Write on page 12 as you think about what you learned.

1. Which job interview tip from Reading 2 do you think is the most important? Which is the hardest to do? Why?

2. In your opinion, what is the best way to make a job interviewer interested in you?

B. Before you watch the video, discuss the questions in a group.

1. What are three things you should do when you begin an interview for a new job?

2. What things should you do after your interview for a new job?

 C. Go online to watch the video about job interviewing skills. Then check your comprehension.

> **common ground** (n.) opinions or interests shared by two or more people
>
> **generic** (adj.) describing a general type of something, not one thing in particular
>
> **rattle through** (phr. v.) to say something very quickly
>
> **scale** (v.) to observe

VIDEO VOCABULARY

D. Think about the unit video, Reading 1, and Reading 2 as you discuss the questions. Then choose one question and write a paragraph in response.

1. What are the best ways to make a good impression on others?

2. Can you make a good first impression the same way in every situation (e.g., at a job interview, talking to a customer, meeting a new classmate, etc.)? Why or why not?

Vocabulary Skill	Using the dictionary to identify word forms

Learning word forms increases your vocabulary. It will help make your reading, speaking, and writing more fluent. Look at the dictionary definitions below.

ac·com·plish /əˈkɑmplɪʃ/ *verb* [T] to succeed in doing something difficult that you planned to do: *Very little was accomplished at the meeting.* **SYN** **achieve**

ac·com·plished /əˈkɑmplɪʃt/ *adj.* highly skilled at something: *an accomplished swimmer*

ac·com·plish·ment /əˈkɑmplɪʃmənt/ *noun* **1** [C] something difficult that someone has succeeded in doing or learning: *He was proud of his academic accomplishments.* **2** (*formal*) [U] the act of completing something successfully

All dictionary entries are from the *Oxford American Dictionary for learners of English* © Oxford University Press 2011.

A. Complete this chart. An *X* indicates that a word form doesn't exist or you don't need to know it at this time. Use your dictionary to help you.

	Noun	Verb	Adjective	Adverb
1.	accomplishment	*accomplish*	*accomplished*	X
2.			considerable	considerably
3.	confidence	X		
4.		demonstrate		X
5.		impress		
6.		offend		
7.		X	responsible	
8.		select		

Tip for Success

Many words have the same noun and verb form. For example, *tie* can be a noun or a verb.

B. Complete each sentence with a word from the chart in Activity A.

1. My biggest ___accomplishment___ in life so far has been my graduation from high school.

2. Appearance is an important _____ if you want to make a good impression. Think carefully about how you will look to others.

3. When you speak in public, you need to show _____. Even if you are nervous, you should look as if you are not.

4. Keeping eye contact will _____ to others that you are interested in what they are saying.

5. The person who applied for the job had a(n) _____ work history. The manager was surprised at the high-level positions she had held.

6. Don't tell jokes when you meet people for the first time because you might _____ them and make them angry or upset.

C. Choose two sets of words from Activity A. Write one sentence for each form of the word. Then share your sentences with a partner.

iQ ONLINE **D.** Go online for more practice with using the dictionary to identify word forms.

WRITING

UNIT OBJECTIVE ▶▶▶▶ At the end of this unit, you will write a paragraph about how to make a good first impression. This paragraph will include specific information from the readings and your own ideas.

Writing Skill   *Part 1*   Organizing and developing a paragraph

A paragraph should discuss one main idea from beginning to end and develop the main idea with specific details.

- The **topic sentence** is usually the first sentence of a paragraph. It identifies the topic, or subject, of the paragraph. It also gives the main idea (or controlling idea), which explains what the writer will say about the topic.
- The **supporting sentences** are the middle sentences of a paragraph. They support the topic sentence with two or three smaller ideas, or subtopics. Subtopics are supported with specific details, such as examples, explanations, facts, definitions, and reasons.
- The **concluding sentence** is usually the last sentence of a paragraph. It summarizes the main points of the paragraph and restates the topic sentence, but in different words.

A. **WRITING MODEL** Read the model paragraph. Then answer the questions on page 20.

How to Annoy Your Coworkers

When you start a job, you can leave a bad impression on your new coworkers very quickly without even realizing it. Because the workplace can be fast-paced and stressful, it can be easy to forget the people around you. One sure way to annoy your coworkers is to speak loudly on your phone. Speaking loudly on the phone can make it difficult for your coworkers to focus on what they are doing or to have phone conversations of their own. It may also send a message that you think your work and phone conversations are more important than anyone else's. Another common mistake is to take the last cup of coffee and not make another pot. Leaving an empty coffee pot means that the next person has to take the time to make a new pot of coffee. Nobody likes to do this, particularly first thing in the morning! Many people find this behavior very rude. Leaving your cell phone on is another way you could unknowingly irritate your coworkers and cause them to form a bad impression of you. Your ringing cell phone may disturb the quiet your coworkers need to do their work. The noise may cause them to work more slowly or make mistakes. Also, many people consider it disrespectful. Finding your dream job may take a lot of time and effort, but unfortunately, leaving a bad impression on your coworkers can be done quickly and easily!

---

1. What is the topic sentence of the paragraph? Circle it.

2. How many supporting sentences are in the paragraph? ____

3. The paragraph gives three ways to make a bad impression on your coworkers. What are these three subtopics? Write them below.

   a. _____

   b. _____

   c. _____

4. The paragraph uses reasons to support the subtopics. What reason explains why a ringing phone may cause people to make mistakes?

   _____

5. What is the concluding sentence of the paragraph? Underline it.

B. Complete the paragraph below. Choose the correct topic sentence and supporting details from the box. Use the information from Reading 1 on pages 6–7 to develop your ideas. One sentence will not be used.

a. Find a shared interest or talk about what is around you, like your school or your teacher.

b. Friends are easy to make at work.

c. There are several ways to make new friends.

d. For example, you could talk about your boss or your customers.

Making New Friends

____ First, if you go to school, you can make new friends in class. Come
 1
early so you have time to meet other people before class starts, and try not to

sit by yourself. Instead, sit next to another student and use small talk to start a

conversation. ____ Soon you will discover what you have in common, and your
            2
new friendship can develop! Another great place to make new friends is at work.

You and your coworkers will already have many things in common to talk about.

____ If your friendship develops, you might even hang out, which will give you
 3
something to look forward to after you finish work. Making new friends is not

always easy, but with a little effort, you can build friendships with the people

around you, and in the process, you may even find your new best friend!

An **outline** is a plan you make before you start writing. Outlines help you put your ideas in order. When you write an outline for a paragraph, include the topic sentence, the subtopics, important supporting details, and the concluding sentence.

Example of an outline

1. **Topic sentence:** When you start a job, you can leave a bad impression on your new coworkers very quickly without even realizing it.
2. **Subtopics and supporting details:**
   A. talking loudly on your phone
      1. coworkers can't focus or have phone calls
      2. sends a message
   B. taking the last cup of coffee
      1. someone else has to make more
      2. many people find it rude
   C. leaving cell phone on
      1. coworkers may work more slowly or make mistakes
      2. many people consider it disrespectful
3. **Concluding sentence:** Finding your dream job may take a lot of time and effort, but unfortunately, leaving a bad impression on your coworkers can be done quickly and easily!

A. [WRITING MODEL] **Read the model paragraph. Then complete the outline on page 22.**

Fixing a Negative Impression

Sometimes we say something that leaves people with a bad impression, but it is possible to fix the situation. First, you must figure out why you have made others upset or uninterested. Think about the conversation you had earlier and try to remember what you said that offended others. For example, sometimes we tell a joke that they do not think is funny. Second, be prepared for the next time you see them. Make a plan about what you want to say and what topics you should avoid. You do not want to make the same mistake twice! Finally, when you see them again, be positive and act interested. Do not bring up the bad past experience. Instead, focus on the present. You should get them to talk a lot so that they feel more comfortable around you. Ask questions, listen carefully to their answers, and respond with thoughtful comments that show you care about what they have to say. There is no standard formula to turn a negative impression into a positive one; however, if you stay positive and seem interested in changing their opinion about you, you are more likely to get them to like you the next time!

1. Topic sentence: <u>Sometimes we say something that leaves people with a</u> <u>bad impression, but it is possible to fix the situation.</u>

2. Subtopics and supporting details:

   A. _____

      1. <u>Think about the conversation.</u>

      2. _____

   B. <u>Be prepared.</u>

      1. _____

      2. _____

   C. _____

      1. <u>Don't bring up the bad past experience.</u>

      2. _____

3. Concluding sentence: _____

_____

_____

_____

Writing **Tip**

Use listing-order transition signals, such as *first*, *second*, and *third*, to introduce subtopics in a paragraph that gives steps or advice.

B. Work with a partner or group to complete this outline for the paragraph in Activity B on page 20. Fill in the topic sentence, the remaining subtopic and supporting details, and a concluding sentence. Use your own ideas.

1. Topic sentence: _____

_____

2. Subtopics and supporting details:

   A. <u>You can make new friends in class.</u>

      1. <u>Come to class early.</u>

      2. _____

      3. _____

   B. _____

      1. _____

      2. _____

3. Concluding sentence: _____

_____

_____

_____

iQ ONLINE   **C.** Go online for more practice with organizing and developing a paragraph.

Grammar	Real conditionals: present and future

The **present real conditional** is used to talk about general truths, habits, and things that happen again and again. It is formed by using the simple present in both the *if* clause (the condition) and the result clause.

if clause	result clause

If you **walk** in wearing jeans and a T-shirt, you **are not likely** to get the position.

You can also use a modal (*may, might, would, could*) in the result clause.

if clause	result clause

If you **disagree** too much in your first conversation, the other person **may think** you are hard to get along with.

The **future real conditional** is used to talk about what will happen under certain conditions. The *if* clause gives the condition. The result clause gives the result. The future real conditional is formed by using the simple present in the *if* clause and the future with *will* or *be going to* in the result clause.

if clause	result clause

If you **smile** frequently, it **will make** other people more comfortable.

if clause	result clause

If you **stay** honest and professional, you **will get** one step closer to the job you want.

You can also use *when* or *whenever* instead of *if* for both the present real conditional and the future real conditional.

when clause	result clause

When you **take care of** yourself, you **feel** better!

result clause	*when* clause

You'**ll impress** other people when you **practice** good listening skills.

A. Underline the *if* or *when* clause and circle the result clause.

1. People want to be around you when you have good listening skills.

2. If you tell a joke, you could offend someone.

3. When you dress appropriately, people take you seriously.

4. You are more likely to make a good impression if you are confident and prepared.

5. If you don't ask questions, people may not think you're interested in what they're saying.

B. Complete each sentence with the correct form of the verb in parentheses. There may be more than one correct answer.

1. If they offer me the job, I think I _____will take_____ it. (take)

2. I _____ better when I exercise regularly. (feel)

3. If a student pays attention in class, the teacher _____ a good first impression of her or him. (have)

4. If you _____ unprepared, the interviewer might think you are not serious. (come)

5. He probably won't pass if he _____. (not, study)

C. Complete each sentence with your own ideas.

1. If you don't get enough sleep, _____.

2. If you don't prepare for the interview, _____.

3. If you don't pay attention to your friend, _____

_____.

4. If you tell a joke, _____.

5. If you arrive 15 minutes late to a job interview, _____

_____.

D. Go online for more practice with real conditionals.

E. Go online for the grammar expansion.

In this assignment, you are going to organize, develop, and write a "how to" paragraph. As you prepare your paragraph, think about the Unit Question, "How do you make a good first impression?" Use information from Reading 1, Reading 2, the unit video, and your work in this unit to support your "how to" paragraph. Refer to the Self-Assessment checklist on page 26.

Go to the Online Writing Tutor for a writing model and alternate Unit Assignments.

PLAN AND WRITE

A. BRAINSTORM **Follow these steps to help you organize your ideas.**

1. Look at the topics and add your own idea. Then choose one of the topics to write about.

How to make a good first impression on:	
a classmate	a college roommate
a teacher	a friend's parents
a new neighbor	your idea: _____

2. Think about your topic and write it here. Brainstorm some things you should do or should not do to make a good first impression. Make a list of dos and don'ts in the T-chart below.

My topic: _____

Dos	Don'ts

B. PLAN Follow these steps to plan your paragraph.

1. Look at the Dos and Don'ts you wrote in Activity 2 on page 25. Circle three ideas you want to use in your paragraph. These are your subtopics.

2. Brainstorm specific examples and reasons for your paragraph. Use ideas from Reading 1, Reading 2, and the unit video to help support your subtopics.

 3. Go to the Online Resources to download and complete the outline for your "how to" paragraph.

 **C.** WRITE Use your PLAN notes to write your paragraph. Go to *iQ Online* to use the Online Writing Tutor.

1. Write your "how to" paragraph on making a good first impression. Be sure to include a topic sentence, supporting sentences, and a concluding sentence.

2. Look at the Self-Assessment checklist below to guide your writing.

REVISE AND EDIT

 **A.** PEER REVIEW Read your partner's paragraph. Then go online and use the Peer Review worksheet. Discuss the review with your partner.

B. REWRITE Based on your partner's review, revise and rewrite your paragraph.

C. EDIT Complete the Self-Assessment checklist as you prepare to write the final draft of your paragraph. Be prepared to hand in your work or discuss it in class.

Yes	No	SELF-ASSESSMENT
☐	☐	Does the paragraph have a strong topic sentence and concluding sentence?
☐	☐	Are there three subtopics with specific details?
☐	☐	Does the paragraph include conditionals? Are they used correctly?
☐	☐	Are all words used in their correct form?
☐	☐	Does the paragraph include vocabulary from the unit?
☐	☐	Did you check the paragraph for punctuation, spelling, and grammar?

D. REFLECT Go to the Online Discussion Board to discuss these questions.

1. What is something new you learned in this unit?

2. Look back at the Unit Question—How do you make a good first impression? Is your answer different now than when you started the unit? If yes, how is it different? Why?

TRACK YOUR SUCCESS

Circle the words you have learned in this unit.

Nouns
accomplishment
confidence 🔑
research 🔑 AWL
slang
stranger 🔑
weakness 🔑

Verbs
appreciate 🔑 AWL
consider 🔑
demonstrate 🔑 AWL
exaggerate 🔑
expect 🔑
impress 🔑
maintain 🔑 AWL
select 🔑 AWL

Phrasal Verb
lead to 🔑

Adjectives
effective 🔑
offensive 🔑
professional 🔑 AWL
punctual
responsible 🔑

🔑 Oxford 3000™ words
AWL Academic Word List

Check (✓) the skills you learned. If you need more work on a skill, refer to the page(s) in parentheses.

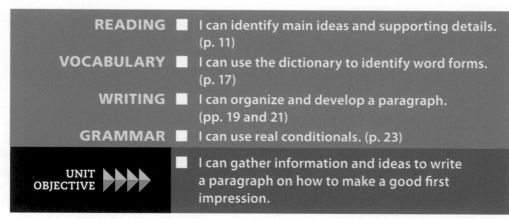

READING ■ I can identify main ideas and supporting details. (p. 11)

VOCABULARY ■ I can use the dictionary to identify word forms. (p. 17)

WRITING ■ I can organize and develop a paragraph. (pp. 19 and 21)

GRAMMAR ■ I can use real conditionals. (p. 23)

UNIT OBJECTIVE ▶▶▶▶ ■ I can gather information and ideas to write a paragraph on how to make a good first impression.

READING	▶	previewing a text
VOCABULARY	▶	use of context to understand words
WRITING	▶	using descriptive adjectives
GRAMMAR	▶	use and placement of adjectives

UNIT QUESTION

What makes food taste good?

A Discuss these questions with your classmates.

1. What kinds of food do you eat every day?

2. What kinds of food do you eat on special occasions?

3. Look at the photo. Do you think how food looks—its presentation—affects how it tastes? Explain.

B Listen to *The Q Classroom* online. Then answer these questions.

1. Yuna says that homemade food tastes the best. Why does homemade food taste better than prepared food?

2. Felix believes foods with too much sugar and fat cause weight problems. In contrast, what kinds of food do you think help people lose weight?

 C Go to the Online Discussion Board to discuss the Unit Question with your classmates.

UNIT
OBJECTIVE ▶▶▶▶ Read the articles and gather information and ideas to
write a descriptive paragraph about your favorite dish.

D Take the quiz to discover what tastes you prefer. Circle your answers.

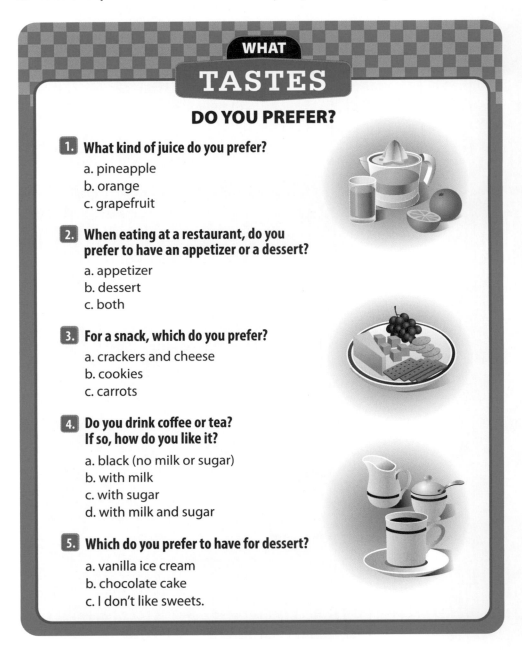

WHAT

TASTES

DO YOU PREFER?

1. **What kind of juice do you prefer?**
a. pineapple
b. orange
c. grapefruit

2. **When eating at a restaurant, do you prefer to have an appetizer or a dessert?**
a. appetizer
b. dessert
c. both

3. **For a snack, which do you prefer?**
a. crackers and cheese
b. cookies
c. carrots

4. **Do you drink coffee or tea? If so, how do you like it?**
a. black (no milk or sugar)
b. with milk
c. with sugar
d. with milk and sugar

5. **Which do you prefer to have for dessert?**
a. vanilla ice cream
b. chocolate cake
c. I don't like sweets.

E Work with a partner. Discuss your answers to the questions in Activity D. Then answer the questions below.

1. Foods can have different tastes. They include sweet, sour, salty, and bitter. What did your answers tell you about the types of foods you prefer?

2. Were your answers very different from your partner's answers? If so, what is one way to explain the differences?

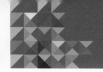
READING 1 | Knowing Your Tastes

You are going to read an article from a food magazine about why people like and dislike certain foods. Use the article to gather information and ideas for your Unit Assignment.

PREVIEW THE READING

A. **PREVIEW** Read the title and headings. Then look at the pictures. The author has two main reasons for writing the article. Check (✓) the two reasons.

☐ to describe different kinds of foods

☐ to compare different kinds of tasters

☐ to argue why people should eat well

☐ to give advice about people's food choices

☐ to explain the causes of overeating

B. **QUICK WRITE** What is an important food or dish in your culture? Write for 5–10 minutes in response. Be sure to use this section for your Unit Assignment.

C. **VOCABULARY** Check (✓) the words you know. Then work with a partner to locate each word in the reading. Use clues to help define the words you don't know. Check your definitions in the dictionary.

balanced *(adj.)*	be made up of *(phr. v.)*	sensitive *(adj.)* 🔑
identify *(v.)* 🔑	recognize *(v.)* 🔑	system *(n.)* 🔑
likely *(adj.)* 🔑	at risk *(phr.)*	typically *(adv.)* 🔑

🔑 Oxford 3000™ words

 **D.** Go online to listen and practice your pronunciation.

A. Read the article and gather information about what makes food taste good.

Knowing Your Tastes

Food Likes and Dislikes

1   Why do some people love spicy food and others hate it? Why do many people dislike broccoli? Why do some people want sweets all the time? Human taste is not as simple as liking or disliking something. The kind of tongue you have can affect your food choices—and your health.

How the Tongue Works

2   The human tongue **is made up of** a group of muscles and taste buds that work together to **recognize** taste. The average adult tongue has 10,000 taste buds, which are tiny bumps located on the tongue. Tiny hairs on the end of the taste buds tell us whether food is sweet, sour, bitter, or salty. The taste buds send messages to the brain as chemicals from the food enter the nose. Together, the taste buds and nose tell the brain exactly what the tongue is tasting. This complex **system** helps humans survive by recognizing which foods are safe and which might be dangerous.

Nontasters, Medium Tasters, Supertasters

3   Although all humans have taste buds, we do not all have the same number of them. *Medium tasters* **typically** have 10,000 taste buds. These "average tasters" make up about 50 percent of the world population. *Nontasters*, 25 percent of the population, have half the

number of taste buds as medium tasters. The remaining 25 percent are *supertasters*. Supertasters have four to six times as many taste buds as nontasters and twice as many as medium tasters (see Figure 1). Research shows that supertasters are more **likely** to be women and from Asia, Africa, and South America.

Different Worlds for Different Tasters

4   Supertasters live in a very colorful world of tastes, nontasters live in a gray world, and medium tasters are somewhere between the two. Supertasters think that a lot of foods are too strong. In addition to having more taste buds, supertasters are born with a gene[1] that makes them **sensitive** to bitter foods. Consequently, they dislike broccoli, cauliflower, grapefruit, and even coffee. With more taste buds, they can more easily feel fatty foods in their mouths. As a result, they stay away from high-fat food items like French fries and sweets. They are also very sensitive to pain on the tongue, so they avoid spicy food. Nontasters, on the other hand, experience fewer tastes in general, so they can enjoy hot foods like chili and pepper with much less pain.

Supertasters, Nontasters, and Diet

5   As a rule, humans avoid foods that taste bad and eat foods that give them pleasure. Since supertasters avoid bitter fruits and

[1] **gene:** a part of a cell in a living thing that decides its characteristics

vegetables, their diets are sometimes not **balanced**, which could put them more **at risk** for certain types of cancers. However, they also dislike fatty and sweet foods, so they tend to be thinner and at lower risk for heart disease and diabetes[2]. In contrast, nontasters like foods high in fat because their tongues do not react negatively to them. All people should pay attention to what they eat, but nontasters and supertasters must be more aware of the foods they are consuming or avoiding and find other ways to make up the difference.

What Kind of "Taster" Are You?

6   If you can **identify** which kind of taster you are, you will be able to make more educated choices about your diet. This simple test can show whether you are a nontaster, medium taster, or supertaster. Put a small amount of blue food coloring on your tongue. Take a piece of notebook paper (the kind with three holes punched out), and put one of the holes over your tongue. Your taste buds will look like little pink bumps on your blue tongue. Count how many bumps you see in the hole. If there are 5 bumps or fewer, you are a nontaster. If there are 30 or more, you are a supertaster. If there are between 5 and 30, you're a medium taster.

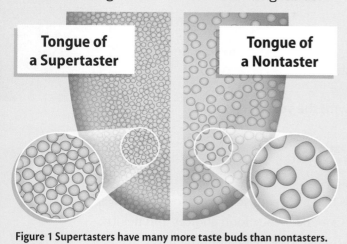

Tongue of a Supertaster

Tongue of a Nontaster

Figure 1 Supertasters have many more taste buds than nontasters.

[2] **diabetes:** a serious disease in which a person's body cannot control the level of sugar in the body

---

Vocabulary Skill Review

In Unit 1, you learned how to identify word forms with a dictionary. Look at all the words in the sentences. Which words are adjectives? Which words are nouns used like adjectives?

B. **VOCABULARY** Complete each sentence with the vocabulary from Reading 1. You may need to change the form of the word or phrase to make the sentence grammatically correct.

balanced (*adj.*)	**be made up of** (*phr. v.*)	**sensitive** (*adj.*)
identify (*v.*)	**recognize** (*v.*)	**system** (*n.*)
likely (*adj.*)	**at risk** (*phr.*)	**typically** (*adv.*)

1. I did not _____ the taste of the cake at first. It took me a minute to realize that it tasted like blackberries.

2. Water _____ hydrogen and oxygen.

3. The human digestive _____ includes the mouth and stomach. It helps to change the food we eat into energy.

4. People who don't eat well are more _____ to get sick than people with healthy diets.

5. People who eat healthy foods and exercise _____ have fewer health problems than people who don't.

6. The police used a photograph to _____ the man who stole Anita's wallet.

7. Most health experts agree that a _____ diet should include different types of foods, such as meat, fruits, vegetables, bread, and cheese.

8. People who don't eat well are _____ of getting sick.

9. Abdullah's teeth are very _____ to cold, so he usually drinks water at room temperature.

 C. Go online for more practice with the vocabulary.

D. Circle the answer to each question.

1. What is the main idea of the article?
   a. As a rule, humans eat foods that taste good and avoid foods that taste bad.
   b. The kind of taster you are can affect your food choices and health.
   c. Supertasters live in a colorful world of taste, but nontasters live in a gray world.
   d. Supertasters have about 20,000 taste buds, double the amount that medium tasters have.

2. Which statement is true about taste buds?
   a. They send messages to the tongue.
   b. The average person has 5,000 taste buds.
   c. They are large bumps on the tongue.
   d. They tell the brain how food tastes.

3. Which statement is true about the number of taste buds a person has?
   a. How many taste buds you have has no effect on taste.
   b. The number of taste buds you have can cause you to like or dislike certain foods.
   c. The more taste buds you have, the more you enjoy spicy foods.
   d. People with a lot of taste buds never eat fruits or vegetables.

4. Which statement is true about the three different kinds of tasters?
   a. Finding out what kind of taster you are can help you make important decisions about your diet.
   b. Supertasters are more likely to be men from Asia, Africa, and South America.
   c. You need a complex test to show you what kind of taster you are.
   d. Unlike nontasters and supertasters, medium tasters do not have to care about the kinds of food they eat.

E. Answer the questions. Write the paragraph number where the answer is found. Then discuss your answers with a partner.

1. What four tastes can taste buds identify? Paragraph: ____

   _____

2. How many taste buds do nontasters have? Paragraph: ____

   _____

3. Who is more likely to be a supertaster, a woman from Italy or a woman from Korea? Paragraph: ____

   _____

4. What types of foods do supertasters avoid? Paragraph: ____

   _____

5. Why should supertasters and nontasters pay close attention to the foods they eat? Paragraph: ____

   _____

   _____

   _____

F. Find these sentences in the article. Then circle the answer to each question.

1. (Paragraph 3) Although all humans have taste buds, we do not all have the same number of **them**.

   Who or what does **them** refer to?

   a. humans   b. taste buds   c. nontasters

2. (Paragraph 4) Consequently, **they** dislike broccoli, cauliflower, grapefruit, and even coffee.

   Who or what does **they** refer to?

   a. foods   b. medium tasters   c. supertasters

3. (Paragraph 4) **They** are also very sensitive to pain on the tongue, so **they** avoid spicy food.

   Who or what does **they** refer to?

   a. spicy food   b. supertasters   c. medium tasters

4. (Paragraph 5) However, **they** also dislike fatty and sweet foods, so **they** tend to be thinner and at lower risk for heart disease and diabetes.

    Who does **they** refer to?

    a. nontasters   b. medium tasters   c. supertasters

5. (Paragraph 5) In contrast, nontasters like foods high in fat because their tongues do not react negatively to **them**.

    Who or what does **them** refer to?

    a. high-fat foods   b. nontasters   c. taste buds

Critical Thinking Tip

Activity G asks you to make **inferences**. When you make an inference, you are guessing that something is true based on what you read and your own knowledge.

G. **Answer these questions. Then compare your answers with a partner.**

1. Medium tasters have about 10,000 taste buds. How many taste buds do supertasters have?

    _____

2. Can people decide to be a supertaster? Why or why not?

    _____

3. Supertasters do not enjoy bitter foods or foods high in fat. They also dislike sweet foods. What kinds of foods do you think supertasters like to eat?

    _____

4. Nontasters like spicy foods and high-fat foods. What kinds of health risks do you think nontasters have because of their diet?

    _____

 **H.** **Go online to read *The Grapefruit Diet* and check your comprehension.**

 # WRITE WHAT YOU THINK

A. **Discuss these questions in a group.**

1. Do you think you are a nontaster, medium taster, or supertaster? Why?

2. What foods do you really like or dislike? Choose one food and describe what you like or dislike about it.

3. In addition to the type of tasters they are, what are other possible reasons why people like certain foods and don't like others?

Writing Tip

Remember to use your topic sentence to state your main idea.

B. **Choose one question and write a paragraph in response. Look back at your Quick Write on page 31 as you think about what you learned.**

Previewing means looking through a text quickly to find the topic and main ideas before you read the whole text. Previewing gives you a general understanding of the reading first, which will help you when you read the whole text from beginning to end. When you preview, the goal is to predict what the text is going to talk about.

Previewing usually includes these steps:

- reading the title and subtitles
- reading the first and last paragraphs
- looking at the photographs and pictures

After you preview a text, you should be able to answer these questions:

- What is the topic of the reading?
- What ideas are discussed in the reading?

A. Look at Reading 2. Follow these steps as you preview the text.

Step 1: Read the title and subtitles.

1. What is the title of the reading? _____

2. There are four headings within the reading. What are they?

   Food, Balance, and Culture; _____

   _____

Step 2: Look at the photographs and pictures.

Look at the photo and picture. What are they of?

_____

Step 3: Read the first and last paragraphs.

Read the paragraphs quickly. Underline the topic sentence of each paragraph.

B. What is the topic of the reading?

_____

C. What ideas are discussed in the reading?

_____

_____

 D. Go online for more practice previewing a text.

READING 2 | Finding Balance in Food

You are going to read an article from an online journal about how culture can affect people's food choices. Use the article to gather information and ideas for your Unit Assignment.

PREVIEW THE READING

A. **PREVIEW** What do you already know about this topic? Share your ideas with a partner.

B. **QUICK WRITE** What is your definition of a balanced diet? Write for 5–10 minutes in response. Be sure to use this section for your Unit Assignment.

C. **VOCABULARY** Work with a partner to find the words in the reading. Circle clues in the text that help you understand the meaning of each word. Then use a dictionary to define any unknown words.

concept (n.) 🔑	method (n.) 🔑	principle (n.) 🔑
consume (v.)	portion (n.)	property (n.) 🔑
cuisine (n.)	practice (n.) 🔑	region (n.) 🔑
influence (v.) 🔑		

🔑 Oxford 3000™ words

 **D.** Go online to listen and practice your pronunciation.

WORK WITH THE READING

 **A.** Read the article and gather information about what makes food taste good.

Finding Balance in Food

Food, Balance, and Culture

1   Nutritionists around the world often speak about the importance of a balanced diet. A balanced diet usually means eating more fruits, vegetables, and grains and consuming fewer foods high in fat, sugar, and cholesterol. When comparing the food habits of different cultures, however, the definition of a "balanced diet" might also be seen differently. A person's culture can **influence** the way he tries to find balance in the foods he **consumes**. Cultures might view balance differently according to the way a dish tastes, or how a meal is prepared and served. Looking at the **concept** of a "balanced diet" through the eyes of two very different cultures makes it clear that the definition can differ greatly.

Figure 1 France has 22 different regions.

France: Balancing Geography and Portions

2   For the French, balance does not come only from using different kinds of ingredients; enjoying the tastes of the country's many **regions** can also make their diet feel balanced. France is divided into 22 regions. Each region has its own local **cuisine** and food traditions, or what the French call *terroir*. The French embrace[1] all 22 regions and the cuisine produced in each. French cafés, restaurants, and food advertisements often refer to[2] the different regions, and to the fact that French people find pleasure in eating foods from different parts of the country in a search for balance.

3   One can also see balance in the way the French serve their food. A traditional French meal can have from three to seven different courses. It might include an appetizer, a main plate, a side plate, a cheese plate, a salad, and a dessert, which makes it a well-balanced dining experience. Each dish is eaten and enjoyed separately, and **portions** are small. This **practice** has even affected the menus of fast-food chains. Many French people dislike the traditional fast-food meal because it is too simple and quick, so fast-food restaurants in France have changed their menus. Some now include an appetizer, a main dish, a dessert, and a coffee to offer diners the balance they want.

China: Balancing Opposites

4   Like French cuisine, traditional Chinese cooking also tries to find balance, but in a different way. The Chinese believe there are two different types of foods, which work together to create harmony in a dish. According to this **principle**, foods like carrots, water, and tofu are "cool" foods because they decrease body heat. In contrast, foods such as chicken, eggs, and mushrooms are "warm" foods because they increase body heat. When a dish has an equal amount of warm and cool foods together, it is considered balanced. Likewise, opposing cooking **methods** balance dishes. Boiling and steaming are water-based, so they contrast well with frying, an oil-based method.

5   The challenge in traditional Chinese cooking is to prepare and eat meals that balance these opposing **properties**. The Chinese believe

Figure 2 sweet and sour chicken

that achieving this kind of balance can result in improved health. For instance, dishes like beef with broccoli and sweet and sour chicken are considered healthy because they have a mix of foods, colors, flavors, and textures. For the same reason, a warm dish like fried rice might be eaten with a cool fruit such as watermelon. The Chinese believe diseases occur when there are too many cool or warm foods in the

---

[1] **embrace:** to accept something
[2] **refer to:** to talk about

human body. For them, food acts as medicine. A person might have heartburn because he or she is eating too much spicy food. As a result, a doctor might suggest drinking iced tea, a cool drink, to balance the extra warmth.

Different Cultures, Shared Desire

6   France and China have very different cultures, and people in each culture have their own ideas of what constitutes a balanced meal, whether it is tastes, menus, ingredients, eating habits, or nutritional benefits. What connects the two, however, is a shared desire to find some kind of balance. A look at their food preferences also suggests that culture and food are not separate from each other. They are closely related, and their connection can be observed around the world in very different and fascinating ways.

B **VOCABULARY** Here are some words from Reading 2. Cross out the word or phrase that is different from the bold word.

1. People who **consume** too many calories typically gain weight.
    a. take in   b. waste   c. eat

2. The foods we eat as children can **influence** the foods we prefer as adults.
    a. make   b. affect   c. help determine

3. The **concept** behind organic food is that farmers should grow fruits, vegetables, and grains without harmful chemicals.
    a. idea   b. part   c. belief

4. Normandy, a northern **region** of France, is home to many famous cheeses.
    a. area   b. place   c. direction

5. Italian **cuisine** is known for its rich, fresh sauces and its pasta dishes.
    a. history   b. cooking   c. food

6. For dinner, I ate meat, vegetables, and just a small **portion** of dessert.
    a. amount   b. kind   c. quantity

7. The **practice** of eating with one's hands is considered rude in some cultures but polite in others.
    a. action   b. advantage   c. custom

8. A unique **property** of water is taking up more space as ice than as a liquid.
    a. quality   b. characteristic   c. size

9. One **principle** of healthy eating is to read the labels on foods.
    a. basic rule   b. decision   c. belief

10. Various cultures use different **methods** for preparing foods.
    a. problems   b. ways   c. processes

 **C.** Go online for more practice with the vocabulary.

D. Circle the answer to each question.

1. What is the main purpose of the article?
   a. to compare how two cultures find balance in food
   b. to explain why the French do not like fast food
   c. to describe the concepts of "warm" foods and "cool" foods
   d. to argue why people need to find balance in food

2. What is the main idea of paragraph 2?
   a. Each of the 22 regions in France has its own *terroir*.
   b. In France, balance comes from eating foods from different regions.
   c. The French find pleasure in eating at different kinds of restaurants.
   d. France's food regions are often mentioned in advertisements.

3. What is the main idea of paragraph 3?
   a. Many French people do not like to eat at fast-food restaurants.
   b. Some fast-food restaurants in France offer three-course meals.
   c. A traditional French meal might include a cheese plate and a dessert.
   d. The French balance their meals by serving many small courses.

4. What is the main idea of paragraph 4?
   a. Opposing foods and cooking methods create balance in Chinese cooking.
   b Cool foods decrease body heat, whereas warm foods increase body heat.
   c The Chinese use both direct heat and water-based cooking methods.
   d. According to the Chinese, eggs decrease body heat.

5. What is the main idea of paragraph 5?
   a. Preparing dishes that balance foods, colors, and flavors is difficult.
   b Warm dishes like fried rice can be balanced with cool fruits.
   c Meals that balance opposing qualities can improve health.
   d. Healthy dishes include beef and broccoli and sweet and sour chicken.

E. Read the statements. Write *T* (true) or *F* (false). Then correct each false statement to make it true.

_____ 1. *Terroir* means local food and food traditions.

_____ 2. There are no fast-food restaurants in France.

_____ 3. French meals always have seven courses.

_____ 4. Some fast-food restaurants in France offer multiple courses.

_____ 5. The French prefer to eat small portions of food.

_____ 6. Carrots and tofu decrease body heat.

_____ 7. Eggs and mushrooms are considered cool foods.

_____ 8. Boiling and frying are opposing cooking methods.

Critical Thinking **Tip**

Activity F asks you to use a **Venn diagram**. A Venn diagram helps you to see similarities and differences between two topics.

F. Look at a student's notes from Reading 2 in the box. Write the student's ideas in the Venn diagram below to compare French and Chinese cuisine.

~~balance of different food regions~~	food preferences affected by culture
balance of warm and cool foods	opposing cooking methods
search for balance	several courses
food as medicine	small portions

French cuisine　　　　**Chinese cuisine**

1. balance of different food regions

Similarities

6.

4.

2.

7.

5.

3.

8.

Tip for Success

Use *because* to show cause-effect relationships. When *because* begins a sentence, put a comma between the two clauses.

G. Identify cause-effect relationships in the reading. Complete the sentences in your own words.

1. Because the French prefer eating several courses,

   <u>fast-food restaurants have changed their menus.</u>

2. Because traditional fast food is very simple and quick,

   _____.

3. The French eat small portions because

   _____.

4. Tofu decreases body heat because _____.

5. Because sweet and sour chicken has a balance of foods, colors, flavors, and textures, _____.

6. Iced tea can relieve heartburn from spicy foods because

_____.

H. Check (✓) the statements you can infer from the reading.

☐ 1. The French are proud of their cuisine.

☐ 2. The French prefer long meals.

☐ 3. French meals are always healthy.

☐ 4. The Chinese believe spicy foods are unhealthy.

☐ 5. A traditional Chinese dish might be fried chicken with steamed vegetables.

WRITE WHAT YOU THINK

A. Discuss the questions in a group. Look back at your Quick Write on page 38 as you think about what you learned.

1. Do you prefer to eat more variety but smaller portions of food, or less variety but bigger portions? Why?

2. What foods do you enjoy from cultures other than your own? How are they different from the foods you grew up with?

B. Before you watch the video, discuss the questions in a group.

1. What spices are popular in your country?

2. Why do you think spicy foods are becoming more popular in the United States?

C. Go online to watch the video about spices. Then check your comprehension.

aroma *(n.)* a smell (usually one that is pleasant)

crave *(v.)* to want and need to have something very much

diverse *(adj.)* very different from each other

melting pot *(n.)* a place where large numbers of people from different countries live together

VIDEO VOCABULARY

D. Think about the unit video, Reading 1, and Reading 2 as you discuss the questions. Then choose one question and write a paragraph in response.

1. What makes food taste good to you?

2. Which foods did you dislike as a child? Which foods do you dislike as an adult? Why do you think food preferences change as you get older?

Vocabulary Skill	Use of context to understand words

Learning to read without stopping to look up new words can help you read faster and understand more. When reading, try to guess the meaning of a new word from **context**. Context refers to the other words and ideas in the sentence that are around the new word:

> A balanced diet usually means eating more fruits, vegetables, and grains and **consuming** fewer foods high in fat, sugar, and cholesterol.

The context around the word *consuming* suggests that the sentence is about what kinds of food to eat and not eat in order to have a balanced diet. Therefore, you can guess that *consuming* has a similar meaning to *eating*.

If you need to know what a word means, start by guessing from the context. If a sentence does not give enough context, then look the word up in the dictionary.

A. Read each sentence and try to answer the question that follows. (The underlined words are for Activity B.)

1. People in every culture have their own ideas of what <u>constitutes</u> a balanced meal, whether it is tastes, menus, ingredients, eating habits, or nutritional benefits.

   What things can make a balanced meal?

   tastes, menus, ingredients, eating habits, and nutritional benefits

2. Beef with broccoli and sweet and sour chicken are two famous <u>dishes</u> that can be found in most Chinese restaurants.

   What foods are common in Chinese restaurants?

   _____

3. Cultures might <u>view</u> balance differently according to the way a dish tastes, or how a meal is prepared and served.

   In what ways can cultures find balance in food?

   _____

4. Nontasters have a <u>taste</u> for sugary foods, which means they eat sweets more often than other people.

Why do nontasters eat sweets?

_____

5. French cheeses can have different <u>textures</u>, from soft cheeses like Brie to hard cheeses like cantal.

In what way can French cheeses differ?

_____

6. In traditional Chinese cooking, foods are in <u>harmony</u> when there is an equal amount of cool and warm foods together.

What foods work together in Chinese cooking?

_____

B. Check (✓) the word or phrase that is closest in meaning to each underlined word from Activity A. Look at the context to help you.

1. constitutes
   - ☐ eats
   - ☐ makes

3. view
   - ☐ think about
   - ☐ eliminate

5. textures
   - ☐ ways that things feel
   - ☐ ways that things smell

2. dishes
   - ☐ meals
   - ☐ tastes

4. taste
   - ☐ an idea
   - ☐ a liking

6. harmony
   - ☐ a good recipe
   - ☐ a good combination

C. Choose four words from Activities A and B. Write a sentence using each word.

1. _____

2. _____

3. _____

4. _____

 **D.** Go online for more practice with the use of context to understand words.

WRITING

UNIT OBJECTIVE ▶▶▶▶ At the end of this unit, you will write a paragraph about your favorite dish using descriptive adjectives. This paragraph will include specific information from the readings and your own ideas.

Writing Skill   Using descriptive adjectives

Adjectives are words that describe nouns (*people, places, things*, and *ideas*). Writers use a lot of adjectives in order to make their descriptions both interesting and clear. They describe what they *see, hear, smell, taste, touch*, and *feel*. They create a picture with words so that readers can easily imagine or "see" what they are describing. Using **descriptive adjectives** in your writing will make it more interesting for the reader.

Non-descriptive: I ate a meal at a restaurant downtown.
Descriptive: I ate a **delicious**, **savory** meal at a **cozy French** restaurant downtown.

A. **WRITING MODEL** Read the model paragraph. Then answer the questions on page 47.

My Mother's Yorkshire Pudding

Whenever I think of my mother's cooking, I always remember her delicious Yorkshire puddings. Although I grew up in the United States, my mother often cooked dishes from her home country of England. She has always been an excellent cook, and one of her best recipes is called Yorkshire pudding, which is a traditional English pastry. It is a simple dish made with eggs, flour, and milk. My mother's Yorkshire puddings taste so good because they are light, crisp, and slightly sweet. She serves them with delicious warm gravy, but I prefer them sweet with strawberry jam.

They are very special because she only serves them on holidays. My sister and I always fight for the last one because they are so delicious. I have had many other people's Yorkshire puddings, but my mother's have always tasted better. Not only are hers homemade, but they also have a special taste that always makes me think of her. In addition, they make me remember my British ancestry and my mother's history. They help me connect to my past and to my family. Yorkshire pudding is such a simple and common English food, but it will always be special to me because of my mother.

1. What is the topic sentence? Underline it.

2. What is the concluding sentence? Underline it.

3. How does Yorkshire pudding taste? Write a sentence that describes the taste.

   _____

4. What do Yorkshire puddings remind the author of?

   _____

5. Circle the adjectives the writer uses to describe Yorkshire pudding.

B. Look at the author's brainstorming notes. Circle the ideas the author used. Cross out the ideas the author did not use.

(eggs), (flour), & (milk)	homemade
~~bake in the oven~~	British ancestry
crisp and sweet	my grandmother
golden brown	family
holidays	smell buttery
sweet with strawberry jam	New Year's Day
fight with sister	

C. Look again at the author's notes in Activity B. Why do you think the author used some of the ideas but not others?

D. WRITING MODEL Read the model paragraph. Check (✓) the best topic sentence on page 48. Then write it on the lines in the paragraph.

The Best Ceviche

_____

_____

_____

Restaurants all over Lima serve this traditional South American seafood dish. Ceviche is a simple recipe made from fresh raw fish, shrimp, and other seafood. The seafood sits in fresh lemon or lime juice, which makes a broth and "cooks" the meat naturally. Hot chili peppers, raw onions, and a little salt are added to the sour juice to give ceviche its special flavor. The fish is cold and citrusy. Sliced limes and fresh cilantro often garnish the top, which makes the dish very colorful and appetizing. Sometimes people just have the broth as an appetizer because it is so delicious. Since Lima is located on the coast of the South Pacific Ocean, restaurants there have access to fresh fish and seafood every morning, so the ceviche is always exceptional. I enjoy ceviche from Lima's famous restaurants, but it is also a common street food. People make their own ceviche and sell it on the streets of Lima. When I see fellow Peruvians enjoying their street ceviche while walking along city sidewalks, I feel very proud of my country and its food.

☐ Ceviche tastes best in the summer because it is cold and refreshing.

☐ Nothing tastes better than the ceviche in Lima, Peru.

☐ People in Lima, Peru enjoy ceviche in restaurants and on the street.

☐ Lima, the capital of Peru, has many good seafood dishes.

E. Fill in the adjectives the author uses in Activity D to describe the nouns.

1. _____simple_____ recipe   5. _____ limes

2. _____ chili peppers   6. _____ cilantro

3. _____ onions   7. _____ restaurants

4. _____ flavor

F. Write your own adjectives to describe each of these nouns from the paragraph in Activity D. Then compare your answers with a partner.

1. _____traditional_____ recipe   4. _____ limes
   _____   _____

2. _____ onions   5. _____ restaurants
   _____   _____

3. _____ flavor
   _____

iQ ONLINE **G.** Go online for more practice with using descriptive adjectives.

Grammar | Use and placement of adjectives

Adjectives are always singular. When two or more adjectives are used before a noun, they usually follow the order given in this chart.

Opinion/ Quality	Size	Age	Shape	Color	Origin	Material	Kind/ Purpose
beautiful	big	old	round	yellow	Chinese	glass	serving
expensive	small	new	square	green	French	leather	running

Rosario lives in a **big, old** house in the country.
We ate dinner at the **new French** restaurant in our neighborhood.
Ming gave Ella and Mike a **beautiful glass serving** dish as a gift.
Eduardo bought a pair of **expensive leather running** shoes.

We do not usually use more than three adjectives before a noun. We use two or three adjectives and then add additional descriptive phrases after the noun.

Leila wore a **beautiful green silk** skirt from India.

A. Write a sentence about each topic with three adjectives from different categories. Use adjectives from the list on page 50 or your own ideas.

1. your favorite dessert _____

_____

2. a member of your family _____

_____

3. something you are wearing today _____

_____

4. something you ate this week _____

_____

5. a DVD or book you like _____

_____

6. a restaurant you like _____

_____

Critical Thinking **Tip**

Activity B asks you to **classify** adjectives. When you classify, you put things into groups according to certain qualities or principles. Classifying information can help you understand it better.

B. Work with a partner. Write each adjective in the correct column of the chart below.

American	friendly	metal	tasty
ancient	funny	modern	teenage
antique	glass	nice	traditional
Brazilian	~~hiking~~	Omani	triangular
ceramic	huge	orange	ugly
~~cheap~~	interesting	oval	uncomfortable
common	jogging	plastic	unusual
cotton	Korean	pretty	wedding
elderly	little	racing	wonderful
elegant	lovely	rectangular	wool
fashionable	medical	silk	writing

Opinion/Quality	cheap,
Size	
Age	
Shape	
Color	
Origin	
Material	
Kind/Purpose	hiking,

C. Go online for more practice with the use and placement of adjectives.

D. Go online for the grammar expansion.

In this assignment, you are going to write a descriptive paragraph about your favorite dish. As you prepare your paragraph, think about the Unit Question, "What makes food taste good?" Use information from Reading 1, Reading 2, the unit video, and your work in this unit to support your descriptive paragraph. Refer to the Self-Assessment checklist on page 52.

Go to the Online Writing Tutor for a writing model and alternate Unit Assignments.

PLAN AND WRITE

A. BRAINSTORM Follow these steps to help you organize your ideas.

1. Think about your favorite dish. Use these questions to help brainstorm ideas about your topic.

   a. What is the name of your dish? _____

   b. How would you describe your dish? What taste(s) and ingredients does it have? _____

   _____

   c. Does this dish have personal or cultural importance to you? Why?

   _____

   _____

   d. Who usually makes this dish for you? Is it easy or difficult to make? Why?

   _____

   _____

   e. How does the dish make you feel? _____

   _____

2. Write a topic sentence that names your dish and expresses your main idea.

   _____

   _____

   _____

3. List eight to ten adjectives that describe your dish. Think about how it looks and tastes. _____

_____

B. PLAN **Follow these steps to plan your paragraph.**

1. Look at the ideas you wrote in Activity A on page 51. Circle your best ideas.

2. Look again at your ideas. Circle your best descriptive adjectives. Check the order. Look at the Grammar Skill on pages 49 and 50 to help you.

3. Go to the Online Resources to download and complete the outline for your descriptive paragraph.

C. WRITE **Use your** PLAN **notes to write your paragraph. Go to** *iQ Online* **to use the Online Writing Tutor.**

1. Write your paragraph that describes your favorite dish. Be sure to use adjectives to make your description interesting, clear, and specific.

2. Look at the Self-Assessment checklist below to guide your writing.

REVISE AND EDIT

A. PEER REVIEW **Read your partner's paragraph. Then go online and use the Peer Review worksheet. Discuss the review with your partner.**

B. REWRITE **Based on your partner's review, revise and rewrite your paragraph.**

C. EDIT **Complete the Self-Assessment checklist as you prepare to write the final draft of your paragraph. Be prepared to hand in your work or discuss it in class.**

Yes	No	SELF-ASSESSMENT
☐	☐	Does the paragraph include descriptive adjectives?
☐	☐	Are the adjectives in the correct order?
☐	☐	Does the paragraph include vocabulary from the unit?
☐	☐	Did you check the paragraph for punctuation, spelling, and grammar?

D. REFLECT Go to the Online Discussion Board to discuss these questions.

1. What is something new you learned in this unit?

2. Look back at the Unit Question—What makes food taste good? Is your answer different now than when you started the unit? If yes, how is it different? Why?

TRACK YOUR SUCCESS

Circle the words and phrases you have learned in this unit.

Nouns
concept 🔑 AWL
cuisine
method 🔑 AWL
portion AWL
practice 🔑
principle 🔑 AWL
property 🔑
region 🔑 AWL
system 🔑

Verbs
consume AWL
identify 🔑 AWL
influence 🔑
recognize 🔑

Phrasal Verb
be made up of

Adjectives
balanced
likely 🔑
sensitive 🔑

Adverb
typically 🔑

Phrase
at risk

🔑 Oxford 3000™ words
AWL Academic Word List

Check (✓) the skills you learned. If you need more work on a skill, refer to the page(s) in parentheses.

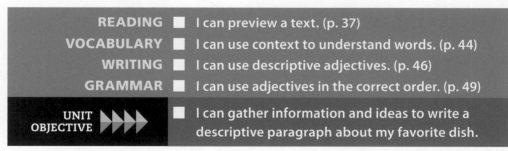

READING	☐ I can preview a text. (p. 37)
VOCABULARY	☐ I can use context to understand words. (p. 44)
WRITING	☐ I can use descriptive adjectives. (p. 46)
GRAMMAR	☐ I can use adjectives in the correct order. (p. 49)
UNIT OBJECTIVE ▶▶▶▶	☐ I can gather information and ideas to write a descriptive paragraph about my favorite dish.

READING ▶ taking notes
VOCABULARY ▶ synonyms
WRITING ▶ writing a summary and a personal response
GRAMMAR ▶ parallel structure

Q?

UNIT QUESTION

How has technology affected our lives?

A Discuss these questions with your classmates.

1. How do you use technology in your daily life?

2. Look at the photo. What kind of technology is the person using? What is he doing?

B Listen to *The Q Classroom* online. Then answer these questions.

1. Sophy says that technology has helped her keep in touch with her friends. What example does she give? Do you agree that technology helps you keep in touch? Why or why or not?

2. Felix, Sophy, Yuna, and Marcus find it hard to imagine life without technology. Do you feel the same way? Can you give an example?

iQ ONLINE **C** Go online to watch the video about technology in the classroom. Then check your comprehension.

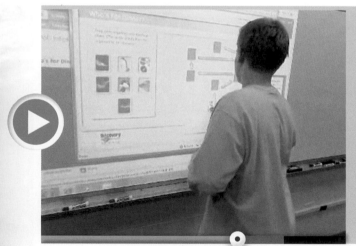

VIDEO VOCABULARY

bucking *(v.)* resisting something

pioneers *(n.)* people who are the first to study something that other people then develop

wind down *(v.)* to reduce in activity as something comes to an end

iQ ONLINE **D** Go to the Online Discussion Board to discuss the Unit Question with your classmates.

E Complete the questionnaire. Think about the tools you use to learn. Which are the most useful? Which are not useful? Check (✓) your opinion. Then discuss your answers with a partner.

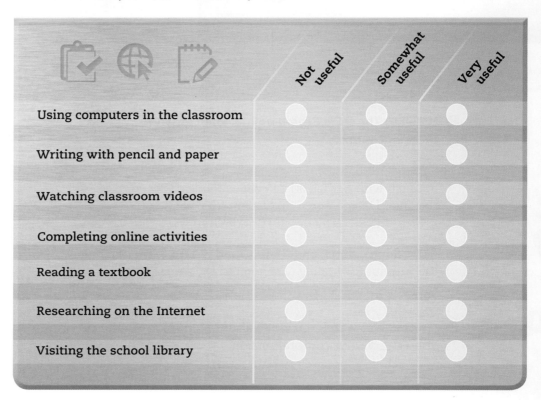

	Not useful	Somewhat useful	Very useful
Using computers in the classroom	◯	◯	◯
Writing with pencil and paper	◯	◯	◯
Watching classroom videos	◯	◯	◯
Completing online activities	◯	◯	◯
Reading a textbook	◯	◯	◯
Researching on the Internet	◯	◯	◯
Visiting the school library	◯	◯	◯

F Discuss these questions in a group.

1. What do you think your classroom will look like in 25 years? What will be different?

2. What would you like to be able to do in your classroom that you can't do now?

READING 1 | Cars That Think

You are going to read an article from an automotive magazine about driverless cars. Use the article to gather information and ideas for your Unit Assignment.

PREVIEW THE READING

A. **PREVIEW** Read the title and first sentence of each paragraph in the article. What is the article's main purpose? Check (✓) your answer.

☐ to show why driverless cars will be too expensive to buy

☐ to suggest that people should buy driverless cars

☐ to discuss advantages and disadvantages of driverless cars

B. **QUICK WRITE** Would you feel comfortable in a driverless car? Why or why not? Write for 5–10 minutes in response. Be sure to use this section for your Unit Assignment.

C. **VOCABULARY** Check (✓) the words you know. Then work with a partner to locate each word in the reading. Use clues to help define the words you don't know. Check your definitions in the dictionary.

benefit (n.) 🔑	obstacle (n.)
data (n.) 🔑	occur (v.) 🔑
limitation (n.)	respond (v.) 🔑
manufacturer (n.) 🔑	sense (v.) 🔑
obey (v.) 🔑	

🔑 Oxford 3000™ words

D. Go online to listen and practice your pronunciation.

WORK WITH THE READING

A. Read the article and gather information about how technology has affected our lives.

Cars That Think

1   Thanks to modern technology, humans have less to do. Machines make our coffee in the morning and clean our dishes. Robots do the vacuuming, mop the floors, and mow our yards hands-free. But what would it be like if machines drove our cars for us? What if cars could drive us to work while we read the newspaper or worked on the computer? This may sound like science fiction[1]. In fact, driverless cars are already on the roads, and could soon end up at a dealer near you.

2   Cars today already think for us. GPS navigation systems can give people directions without looking at a map. Sensors[2] built into cars sound an alarm if drivers get too close to a person or another vehicle. Cameras can see for us at night and steer cars around **obstacles** to avoid accidents. By using GPS, sensors, and cameras together, cars can now park themselves and control drivers when they're about to make a dangerous turn.

a prototype driverless car, driving down a road without a driver

Now car companies are building driverless cars that will do all of this, and much more.

3   Driverless cars use a lot of the same technological features to make hands-free driving possible. A prototype[3] driverless car has sensors and cameras to give the car a 360-degree "eye" to **sense** its full environment. The sensors can "see" turns, red lights, stop signs, and other cars. Its computer uses GPS and other **data** to drive the car safely to its destination. All you need to do is tell it where to go and how you want to drive. Select "cautious," and it will **obey** the speed limit. Or choose "aggressive," and drive faster.

4   According to car **manufacturers**, hands-free driving has important **benefits**. For one, driverless cars can improve safety. In the United States, over 90% of car accidents are the result of human error. Drivers can make bad judgments, get sleepy, and run red lights, but robots don't. In a hands-free car, people can **respond** to email without worrying about hitting another car. Also, driverless cars would use less fuel. They don't need to be as heavy because they are less likely to crash.

5   Although driverless cars sound perfect, there are **limitations**. For instance, automated[4] cars cannot anticipate the unexpected like humans can. They might not recognize when a police officer tells traffic to stop or pull off the road. Driverless cars may be too "polite" on the highway, where many people speed. A car that is

---

[1] **science fiction:** books about events that take place in the future

[2] **sensor:** equipment that can detect certain sounds and movements

[3] **prototype:** a model or design of something from which other forms are developed

[4] **automated:** operated by machine, without needing people

following the speed limit could cause more accidents. In addition, if an accident does **occur**, who is to blame? Do you blame the driver? The car? The car manufacturer? Driving laws are written for human drivers, not robots. Therefore, countries will have to decide who is responsible and write new laws, which won't be easy.

6   In the end, consumers will decide if driverless cars are to become the cars of the future. Some might not want to give up control of the wheel. Others may want driving to be as easy as making coffee. Car manufacturers already believe in the driverless car. Prototype driverless cars have already driven over 200,000 miles accident-free, but only time will tell if consumers believe they should.

B. | VOCABULARY | Complete each sentence with the vocabulary from Reading 1.

benefit *(n.)*	**obstacle** *(n.)*
data *(n.)*	**occur** *(v.)*
limitation *(n.)*	**respond** *(v.)*
manufacturer *(n.)*	**sense** *(v.)*
obey *(v.)*	

Vocabulary Skill Review

In Unit 1, you learned how to identify word forms with a dictionary. Circle the nouns and underline the verbs in Activity B.

1. Even though cars have headlights, accidents are more likely to _____ at night because drivers can't see as well.

2. The police expect drivers to _____ the speed limit on highways. If drivers go too fast, they may get a ticket.

3. In many buildings, the lights can _____ when people enter a room, and they turn on by themselves.

4. If my computer turns off by accident, I don't worry about losing my work because the _____ is already saved.

5. The car _____ has decided to build a car that runs on gasoline and electricity because its customers want vehicles that use less fuel.

6. My boss expects me to _____ to his emails right away. If he doesn't hear from me, he gets upset.

7. One _____ of driving to work is that it saves me time, but a disadvantage is that I can get stuck in traffic.

8. If you don't pay for a membership to the website, you can't read all the articles. There's a(n) _____ on how much information you can access without paying.

9. Sand is a real _____ when driving in the desert. It makes it difficult to control the speed and direction of the car.

iQ **ONLINE** **C.** Go online for more practice with the vocabulary.

D. Read the sentences. Then number them in the order that the ideas appear in the article.

____ a. Driverless cars are not perfect machines.

____ b. Today's cars can already do many tasks automatically.

____ c. Car manufacturers believe hands-free driving has advantages.

____ d. The future success of driverless cars will depend on consumers.

____ e. New cars and driverless cars use similar technology.

E. Circle the main idea of the article.
   a. Modern technology is making daily tasks easier for people to do.
   b. Car manufacturers say that driverless cars will use less gasoline.
   c. Driverless cars might cause more accidents on roads and highways.
   d. In the near future, driverless cars may change the way people drive.

F. Answer the questions. Write the paragraph number where the answer is found. Then discuss your answers with a partner.

1. How would driverless cars save fuel?

   Paragraph: _4_

   They can be lighter because they are less likely to crash.

2. How many miles have the prototype cars already driven accident-free?

   Paragraph: ____

   _____

3. What do modern cars use to park themselves?

   Paragraph: ____

   _____

4. What limitations do driverless cars have?

   Paragraph: ____

   _____

   _____

   _____

G. Read the statements. Write *F* (fact) or *O* (opinion).

____ 1. Using a driverless car has several important benefits.

____ 2. Driverless cars are safer than traditional cars.

____ 3. Hands-free driving requires modern technology.

____ 4. Over 90 percent of car accidents in the U.S. are due to human error.

____ 5. Driverless cars use sensors and GPS to navigate.

____ 6. Hands-free driving sounds like science fiction.

____ 7. Driving laws are not written for robots.

____ 8. It will be difficult for countries to write new laws for driverless cars.

H. Complete the graphic organizer using your own words. Identify the advantages and disadvantages of driverless cars. Write the paragraph number where you find your answer.

Advantages of driverless cars	Disadvantages of driverless cars
1. _They can help people stay safe._ Paragraph: _4_	1. _They can't anticipate unexpected_ _things like people can._ Paragraph: ____
2. _They can warn people when there is a_ _dangerous turn._ Paragraph: ____	2. _They cannot recognize police officers._ Paragraph: ____
3. _____ Paragraph: ____	3. _____ Paragraph: ____
4. _____ Paragraph: ____	4. _____ Paragraph: ____
5. _____ Paragraph: ____	5. _____ Paragraph: ____

I. Go online to read *The Superbus* and check your comprehension.

WRITE WHAT YOU THINK

A. Discuss these questions in a group.

1. Why do you think car companies want to make driverless cars?

2. Compare and evaluate the advantages and disadvantages of driverless cars. Would you consider buying a driverless car? Why or why not?

B. Choose one question and write a paragraph in response. Look back at your Quick Write on page 57 as you think about what you learned.

Taking notes while you are reading will help you become a more active reader. To take notes, write on the text and next to the text. Your notes should help you identify important ideas. You should:

- underline or highlight topics and main ideas
- underline supporting details and the most important words and phrases
- focus on content words like nouns, verbs, and adjectives
- summarize the main idea of each paragraph in the margin—don't use complete sentences

Reviewing your notes can help you remember important concepts. Use your notes to prepare for a class or an exam.

A. **Read the second paragraph of Reading 1 below. Look at the student's notes in blue. Then discuss the questions with a partner.**

Cars today already think for us. GPS navigation systems can give people directions without looking at a map. Sensors built into cars sound an alarm if drivers get too close to a person or another vehicle. Cameras can see for us at night and steer cars around obstacles to avoid accidents. By using GPS, sensors, and cameras together, cars can now park themselves and control drivers when they're about to make a dangerous turn. Now car companies are building driverless cars that will do all of this, and much more.

"Smart" cars → safer driving

1. What types of words did the student underline?

2. Look at the words and ideas the student did not underline. Why are they less important?

3. Look at the note in the margin. What does the note summarize?

4. What is the main idea of the paragraph? How do you know?

B. Reread Reading 1. Take notes using ideas from the Reading Skill box and Activity A. Then compare your notes with a partner.

 **C.** Go online for more practice taking notes.

READING 2 | Living Outside the Box

 You are going to read an article from an online newspaper. In the article, the author describes her experiences living without a television for one full winter. Use the article to gather information and ideas for your Unit Assignment.

PREVIEW THE READING

A. **PREVIEW** Read the title and look at the photographs. Do you think the author will say that giving up watching TV was a positive or negative experience? Check (✓) your answer.

☐ positive

☐ negative

B. **QUICK WRITE** How can giving up television affect a person's life positively? Write for 5–10 minutes in response. Be sure to use this section for your Unit Assignment.

C. **VOCABULARY** Work with a partner to find the words in the reading. Circle clues in the text that help you understand the meaning of each word. Then use a dictionary to define any unknown words.

confession (n.)	**experiment** (n.) 🔑	**rare** (adj.) 🔑
discover (v.) 🔑	**lifestyle** (n.)	**regret** (v.) 🔑
eventually (adv.) 🔑	**occasion** (n.) 🔑	**survive** (v.) 🔑

🔑 Oxford 3000™ words

 D. Go online to listen and practice your pronunciation.

WORK WITH THE READING

🔊 **A.** Read the article and gather information about how technology has affected our lives.

Living Outside the Box

1   I once unplugged the TV for a month. It was summer, the season of long walks, barbecues, and reruns. But I knew if I really wanted to prove I could avoid evening television, I'd have to **survive** a New England winter without it. In the darkest, coldest months, I would no longer be able to escape. This winter, I had my test.

2   A year ago I moved into my own place. It was just a few minutes away from my former roommate—and her television. Friends offered me a spare TV, but I said no. Living alone was an opportunity to choose how I wanted to live. And I thought that being TV-free would help me do all those things I wanted to do but didn't have time for.

3   I wondered if I would feel lonely, but decided it would be better not to try to spend time with my "friends" on TV. In the first month or so, I got away from my favorite shows by visiting real friends. **Eventually**, I didn't know what TV shows were on when. I could no longer join in conversations at my office about popular shows.

4   I kept telling people it was an **experiment**: "We'll see how it goes this winter," I'd say. I considered buying a small TV to keep in the closet and bring out on special **occasions**. But for all I was missing, I could feel positive changes. I found myself reading lots of books. I had thought that I was too tired to read after a long day at work, but not too tired to watch TV. Now I had more time to read and sleep. I also started doing volunteer work almost every week instead of every few months. I called friends who usually heard from me only at the holidays. Sometimes I even enjoyed that **rare** thing called quiet.

5   The goal wasn't to give up all entertainment. I can play DVDs on my laptop, so when a blizzard was on its way, I lined up in a video store with everybody else.

Instead of channel-surfing and watching something I would later **regret**, I caught up on some great DVDs. I found myself resensitized[1]. I was no longer watching images without noticing their speed.

6   Sometime during the winter, the season I thought would be the most difficult, I **discovered** I had crossed the line from experiment to **lifestyle**. Finally, I put up a photo on the only living room wall that could have a TV. A friend came over for the first time, took the tour, and then sat down on the couch with a slightly puzzled look. Looking around the room, she asked, "So, don't you have a TV?"

7   Whenever I explain my TV-free home, I tell people I'm not judging anyone else's TV-viewing choices (after all, I'm glad my friends don't mind me sitting in front of their screens every once in a while). The response is often a **confession**. For example, one coworker said she can't help turning her TV on for background noise when her husband is out of town. Others express camaraderie[2], saying they hardly ever turn theirs on.

8   I don't know how long my new lifestyle will last. I might suddenly want to reconnect with contemporary culture and documentaries. And if I have children, I think I'd want them to learn, as I did from my parents, how to view with moderation[3] and a critical[4] eye. But if I do make space for a TV someday, I'm more confident now that I'll still find time and space for me.

[1] **resensitized:** feeling more sensitive or emotional again

[2] **camaraderie:** a feeling of friendship and closeness

[3] **moderation:** the quality of being able to control your feelings or actions

[4] **critical:** describing the good and bad points of a TV show, book, and so on

B. **VOCABULARY** Complete the email with the vocabulary from Reading 2.

confession (n.)	experiment (n.)	rare (adj.)
discover (v.)	lifestyle (n.)	regret (v.)
eventually (adv.)	occasion (n.)	survive (v.)

Vocabulary Skill Review

In Unit 1, you learned about word forms. Some comparative adjectives end in -er. Find and circle them in the email.

To: Megan Morris

From: Laura Jones

Subject: Goodbye cell phone!

Hey Megan,

You haven't heard from me for a while. I'm emailing you because I have lost my cell phone. But don't worry! In fact, I have to make a(n) _____1_____: I don't miss it at all! Losing it allowed me to _____2_____ that I am happier without it! At first, I didn't think I could _____3_____ without having my cell phone always with me. I used to have it with me all the time—even at the beach and in the park. I used it to take photos at every special _____4_____, like my cousin's wedding. I did consider buying a new one at first, but then I thought it would be fun to be one of those _____5_____ people who doesn't own a cell phone. It was my own little _____6_____. I wanted to test myself. _____7_____, I found that I was happier—and safer—without it. I don't text while walking anymore, and I have more time for myself. I don't _____8_____ my decision to live cell-free. In fact, I love my new _____9_____. Talk to you soon—just don't call my cell!

Miss you lots,

Laura

iQ ONLINE **C.** **Go online for more practice with the vocabulary.**

D. Take notes on the main idea of each paragraph in Reading 2. Circle the topic of paragraphs 1–3 below. Then write the topic of paragraphs 4–8.

1. Paragraph 1

   MAIN IDEA: _____

       TOPIC: a. going without TV through winter
                   b. living in New England
                   c. doing summer activities

2. Paragraph 2

   MAIN IDEA: _____

       TOPIC: a. moving into a new home
                   b. living alone without TV
                   c. having time

3. Paragraph 3

   MAIN IDEA: _____

       TOPIC: a. her conversations with coworkers
                   b. her favorite TV shows
                   c. her relationships with people

4. Paragraph 4

   MAIN IDEA: _____

       TOPIC: _____

5. Paragraph 5

   MAIN IDEA: _____

       TOPIC: _____

6. Paragraph 6

   MAIN IDEA: _____

       TOPIC: _____

7. Paragraph 7

   MAIN IDEA: _____

       TOPIC: _____

8. Paragraph 8

   MAIN IDEA: _____

       TOPIC: _____

E. **Look at your notes in Activity D. Circle the main idea of the article.**

    a. When the author became TV-free, her friends offered her a television for her new home, but she decided not to accept.

    b. The author enjoyed reading books, sleeping longer, seeing her friends, and having quiet time.

    c. The author decided to escape from TV as an experiment and eventually came to prefer her new lifestyle.

    d. The author is not sure how long she will live without a television because she might have children in the future.

F. **Read the statements. Write *T* (true) or *F* (false). Then correct each false statement to make it true.**

  _F_ **1.**   She first stopped watching TV in the ~~winter~~. (*summer*)

  ____ **2.**   She considered putting a small TV in her closet.

  ____ **3.**   She still watched DVDs.

  ____ **4.**   She did volunteer work most weeks.

  ____ **5.**   She will teach her children not to watch TV.

  ____ **6.**   She is sure that she will buy a television in the future.

Tip for Success

Use *before* and *after* to show time order. When *before* and *after* begin a sentence, put a comma between the two clauses.

G. **Number the two events to show the correct order. Then combine the two events into a single sentence with *after* or *before*.**

1. a. _2_ Her friends offered her an extra TV.

    b. _1_ She moved to a new home.

    (after) _After she moved to a new home, her friends offered her an extra TV._

2. a. ____ She got home from work.

    b. ____ She had enough energy to read books.

    (after) _____

3. a. ____ She got rid of her TV.

    b. ____ She used to talk with her coworkers about popular TV shows.

    (before)_____

    _____

H. **What do you think the author's life was like before she stopped watching TV? Write 5–8 sentences giving your opinion.**

WRITE WHAT YOU THINK

A. Discuss the questions in a group. Look back at your Quick Write on page 64 as you think about what you learned.

1. Would you consider escaping from television for a month or more? Why or why not?

2. Besides television, what kind of technology would be most difficult for you to live without?

B. Think about the unit video, Reading 1, and Reading 2 as you discuss the questions. Then choose one question and write a paragraph in response.

1. How much control should people have over the technology they use? Why?

2. What positive and negative effects can technology have on people's lives?

Vocabulary Skill   Synonyms

Synonyms are words that have similar meanings. Learning synonyms will increase your vocabulary and will give your writing more variety.

People's <u>lifestyles</u> have changed because of new technology.
People's <u>habits and behaviors</u> have changed because of new technology.

Be careful when choosing synonyms because they do not always have exactly the same meaning. A synonym can have a more general meaning or a more specific meaning.

General: Drivers are expected to <u>follow</u> the rules of the road.
Specific: Drivers are expected to <u>obey</u> the rules of the road.

Follow is more general because it means to do what you are told. *Obey* is more specific because it suggests you *must* do what you are told.

 **for Success**

A **thesaurus** is a book that lists synonyms. Remember that words can have multiple meanings. When you check a thesaurus, make sure you look for the correct synonym for the word.

A. Rewrite each sentence by replacing the bold word or phrase with the correct synonym from the box.

benefits	eventually	limitations	rare
~~data~~	experiments	occurs	

1. The GPS navigation system stores **information** about highway exits and speed limits.

   <u>The GPS navigation system stores data about highway exits and speed limits.</u>

2. When an accident **happens**, the police must decide who is responsible.

   _____

3. Are there any **disadvantages** to using robots and machines for everyday tasks?

   _____

4. It is **unusual** for many people not to use technology in their daily lives.

   _____

5. Researchers have created **tests** that study how driverless cars respond to accidents.

   _____

   _____

6. It may be difficult for consumers to accept driverless cars, but **in the end**, they may become popular because they have many **advantages**.

   _____

   _____

B. Read each pair of sentences. Look at the synonyms in bold. Write *G* next to the sentence that uses a more general synonym. Write *S* next to the one that uses a more specific synonym.

1. a. _G_ Driverless cars may give people the **opportunity** to read while driving.

   b. _S_ Driverless cars may give people the **freedom** to read while driving.

2. a. ___ Sensors can tell the car if an accident **is about to** occur.

   b. ___ Sensors can tell the car if an accident **is going to** occur.

3. a. ___ **I am not upset about** giving up television for a month.

   b. ___ **I don't regret** giving up television for a month.

4. a. ___ The camera can **sense** any obstacle that is in the road.

   b. ___ The camera can **see** any obstacle that is in the road.

5. a. ___ The car will **follow** the driver's instructions.

   b. ___ The car will **obey** the driver's instructions.

 **C.** Go online for more practice with synonyms.

WRITING

UNIT OBJECTIVE ▶▶▶▶ At the end of this unit, you will write a summary paragraph and a personal response paragraph. These paragraphs will include specific information from Reading 2 and your own ideas.

Writing Skill | Writing a summary and a personal response

A **summary** paragraph tells the reader the main ideas of a reading in your own words. A good summary begins by restating the main idea of the reading. It gives a basic outline of the reading and includes supporting details that are necessary to understand the main points. A summary uses synonyms and similar language to restate ideas from the reading.

A summary is often followed by a **personal response** paragraph. A personal response paragraph gives your personal reaction to the reading. It often includes ideas that you agree or disagree with and gives reasons why you agree or disagree.

A. WRITING MODEL Read the model summary and personal response to Reading 1 on pages 58–59. Then answer the questions on page 73.

In the near future, driverless cars may change the way people drive. The cars use technology that is already in many modern cars, such as GPS, sensors, and cameras. The sensors see the road and make decisions about turns and stops, and the GPS navigation system tells the car where to go. Car manufacturers say driverless cars are safer and use less gasoline. However, they cannot understand real-life situations, like obeying police instructions, as well as humans can. Also, it is not clear who is at fault when a driverless car causes an accident. The success of these cars will eventually depend on consumers, not car manufacturers.

I was surprised to read about cars that can drive themselves. To me, it sounds like something from a futuristic movie, not real life. I understand why some people would like to own a driverless car, but I don't agree that they are the cars of the future for two reasons. First of all, I personally think that people would prefer to be in control when driving. People know that they are better at reacting to unexpected situations than a machine. They would feel terrible if their driverless car caused an accident that they could have avoided if they were in control. Also, I think people would worry about the car's computer making mistakes. Computers can shut down, get viruses, and have errors. Nobody wants to experience these problems when they drive.

1. Which sentence summarizes the main idea of the reading? Underline it.

2. Read these sentences from Reading 1. Underline the sentences in the model on page 72 that summarize them.

   a. The sensors can "see" turns, red lights, stop signs, and other cars. Its computer uses GPS and other data to drive the car safely to its destination.

   b. In addition, if an accident does occur, who is to blame? Do you blame the driver? The car? The car manufacturer?

   c. In the end, consumers will decide if driverless cars are to become the cars of the future.

3. Does the writer of the model summary have a positive or negative reaction to driverless cars? How do you know?

   _____

   _____

4. What reasons does the writer give to support her opinions?

   _____

   _____

5. Do you agree with the writer? Why or why not?

   _____

   _____

B. Answer the questions to gather ideas for your summary paragraph about Reading 2 on pages 65–66. Write complete sentences.

1. What was the author's experiment?

   _____

2. How does the author feel about her new lifestyle? Why?

   _____

   _____

3. Why did the author decide to do the experiment?

   _____

   _____

4. What benefits did the experiment have on the author's personal life?

_____

_____

_____

5. What benefits did the experiment have on the author's relationship with friends?

_____

6. What does the author think about her future?

_____

_____

C. Answer the questions to gather ideas for your personal response paragraph about Reading 2. Write complete sentences.

1. What is your personal reaction to the author's decision?

_____

_____

2. Is your reaction positive or negative? Why?

_____

_____

3. Do you agree with the author that living TV-free is a good idea? Why or why not?

_____

_____

iQ ONLINE **D.** Go online for more practice with writing summaries and personal responses.

Parallel structure means using the same word form or grammatical structure to list ideas that come in a sequence. Using parallel structure makes your writing clearer and more effective. Use the conjunctions *and*, *but*, and *or* to connect parallel ideas. Look at the examples of parallel and nonparallel structures.

Parallel: Now I was well read *and* well rested.
               adv. + adj.   adv. + adj.

Not parallel: Now I was well read and getting more rest.

Parallel: Machines make our coffee *and* clean our dishes.
                 verb   verb

Not parallel: Machines make our coffee and our dishes are cleaned.

Parallel: People can tell the car to drive cautiously *or* aggressively.
                                    adv.   adv.

Not parallel: People can tell the car to drive with caution or aggressively.

A. Read these sentences from the readings. Underline the parallel structures and identify the word forms. Circle the conjunctions.

1.   Robots <u>do</u> the vacuuming, <u>mop</u> the floors, (and) <u>mow</u> our yards hands-free.

2.   Sensors built into cars sound an alarm if drivers get too close to a person or another vehicle.

3.   They might not recognize when a police officer tells traffic to stop or pull off the road.

4.   It was summer, the season of long walks, barbecues, and reruns.

5.   I had thought that I was too tired to read after a long day at work, but not too tired to watch TV.

6.   And I thought that being TV-free would help me do all those things I wanted to do but didn't have time for.

7.   Instead of channel-surfing and watching something I would later regret, I caught up on some great DVDs.

Critical Thinking Tip

Activity B asks you to **combine** sentences. Whether you are combining sentences, ideas, or information sources, you are putting things together to make something new. This shows that you understand information and can use it in new ways.

B. Combine each pair of sentences into one. Use *and, but,* or *or* and parallel structure.

1. Her friends were puzzled. They were supportive.

   Her friends were puzzled but supportive.

2. I didn't know what was on TV. I didn't care what was on TV.

   _____

3. People should watch TV with moderation. People should watch with a critical eye.

   _____

4. Do you blame the driver? Do you blame the car? Do you blame the car manufacturer?

   _____

5. Drivers can make bad judgments. They can get sleepy. They can run red lights.

   _____

6. Driverless cars are already on the roads. They could soon end up at a dealer near you.

   _____

   _____

C. Go online for more practice with parallel structure.

D. Go online for the grammar expansion.

In this assignment, you are going to write two paragraphs. In the first paragraph, you will write a summary of Reading 2. In the second paragraph, you will write your personal response about the author's decision and experience of living without TV. As you prepare your paragraphs, think about the Unit Question, "How has technology affected our lives?" Use information from Reading 1, Reading 2, the unit video, and your work in this unit to support your paragraphs. Refer to the Self-Assessment checklist on page 78.

Go to the Online Writing Tutor for a writing model and alternate Unit Assignments.

PLAN AND WRITE

A. BRAINSTORM Follows these steps to help you gather your ideas.

1. For your summary paragraph, write the main idea of Reading 2 in your own words.

   Main idea: _____

2. For your personal response paragraph, write your thoughts about the decisions the author made and her experiences. Think about these questions as you write:

   Are there decisions she made that you agree or disagree with?

   Do you think her experience was positive or negative?

   Did anything in the reading surprise you?

B. PLAN Follow these steps to plan your paragraphs.

1. For your summary paragraph, look at the sentences you wrote in Activity B on pages 73–74. Circle the details that support the main idea.

2. Go to the Online Resources to download and complete the outline for your summary paragraph.

3. For your personal response paragraph, look at the sentences you wrote in Activity C on page 74.

4. Go to the Online Resources to download and complete the outline for your personal response paragraph.

C. WRITE Use your PLAN notes to write your paragraphs. Go to *iQ Online* to use the Online Writing Tutor.

1. Write your summary paragraph first. Then write your personal response paragraph.

2. Look at the Self-Assessment checklist below to guide your writing.

REVISE AND EDIT

A. PEER REVIEW Read your partner's paragraphs. Then go online and use the Peer Review worksheet. Discuss the review with your partner.

B. REWRITE Based on your partner's review, revise and rewrite your paragraphs.

C. EDIT Complete the Self-Assessment checklist as you prepare to write the final draft of your paragraphs. Be prepared to hand in your work or discuss it in class.

SELF-ASSESSMENT		
Yes	No	
☐	☐	Does the summary paragraph give the main idea of Reading 2 and include supporting details?
☐	☐	Does the personal response paragraph include reasons for the writer's opinion?
☐	☐	Are parallel structures used correctly?
☐	☐	Is there a variety of synonyms used?
☐	☐	Do the paragraphs include vocabulary from the unit?
☐	☐	Did you check the paragraphs for punctuation, spelling, and grammar?

D. REFLECT Go to the Online Discussion Board to discuss these questions.

1. What is something new you learned in this unit?

2. Look back at the Unit Question—How has technology affected our lives? Is your answer different now than when you started the unit? If yes, how is it different? Why?

TRACK YOUR SUCCESS

Circle the words you have learned in this unit.

Nouns
benefit 🔑 AWL
confession
data 🔑 AWL
experiment 🔑
lifestyle
limitation
manufacturer 🔑
obstacle
occasion 🔑

Verbs
discover 🔑
obey 🔑
occur 🔑 AWL
regret 🔑
respond 🔑 AWL
sense 🔑
survive 🔑 AWL

Adjective
rare 🔑

Adverb
eventually 🔑 AWL

🔑 Oxford 3000™ words
AWL Academic Word List

Check (✓) the skills you learned. If you need more work on a skill, refer to the page(s) in parentheses.

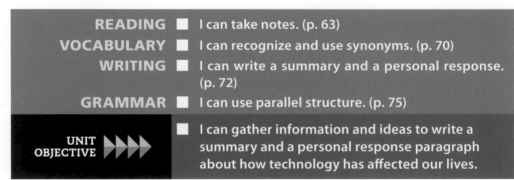

READING	☐ I can take notes. (p. 63)
VOCABULARY	☐ I can recognize and use synonyms. (p. 70)
WRITING	☐ I can write a summary and a personal response. (p. 72)
GRAMMAR	☐ I can use parallel structure. (p. 75)
UNIT OBJECTIVE ▶▶▶▶	☐ I can gather information and ideas to write a summary and a personal response paragraph about how technology has affected our lives.

READING	▶	distinguishing facts from opinions
VOCABULARY	▶	suffixes
WRITING	▶	writing an opinion essay
GRAMMAR	▶	compound sentences

Q?

UNIT QUESTION

Does advertising help or harm us?

A Discuss these questions with your classmates.

1. What items have you purchased because of an advertisement?

2. Has an advertisement ever helped you in some way? What kind of ad was it? How did it help you?

3. Look at the photos. Do you think there is too much advertising around us?

B Listen to *The Q Classroom* online. Then answer these questions.

1. Match each idea in the box to the students in the chart. Then check (✓) if each student thinks advertising helps or harms us.

> a. It makes us want things we don't need.
> b. It gives us information about new products.
> c. It pays for a lot of things I like.
> d. You can't trust the information you get from advertising.

	Does advertising help or harm us?	Helps us	Harms us
Yuna	b. It gives us information about new products.	☑	☐
Felix		☐	☐
Marcus		☐	☐
Sophy		☐	☐

2. Which student do you agree with the most? Can you think of any examples of how advertising helps or harms us to support your ideas?

iQ ONLINE **C** Go to the Online Discussion Board to discuss the Unit Question with your classmates.

D Discuss these questions in a group.

1. Where do you typically see advertisements?

2. Where do you think you might see advertisements like the ones in these photos?

1

2

3

4

Critical Thinking Tip

Activity E asks you to separate the advertisements into **categories** according to purpose. **Categorizing** things helps you notice the way they are similar or different.

E Check (✓) the purpose of each advertisement in Activity D. Some advertisements may have more than one purpose.

	To provide information	To provide help	To sell something
Advertisement 1	☐	☐	☐
Advertisement 2	☐	☐	☐
Advertisement 3	☐	☐	☐
Advertisement 4	☐	☐	☐

READING

READING 1 | Food Advertising Tricks You Should Know About

UNIT OBJECTIVE ▶▶▶▶

You are going to read a magazine article about food advertising. Use the article to gather information and ideas for your Unit Assignment.

PREVIEW THE READING

A. **PREVIEW** Read the title and first paragraph. What is the article's main idea? Check (✓) your answer.

☐ to explain why food looks so different from the photos

☐ to explain what advertisers do to make food look better

☐ to advise people about what foods to eat

B. **QUICK WRITE** Think about a time when an advertisement influenced you. Write for 5–10 minutes in response. Be sure to use this section for your Unit Assignment.

C. **VOCABULARY** Check (✓) the words you know. Then work with a partner to locate each word in the reading. Use clues to help define the words you don't know. Check your definitions in the dictionary.

anticipation *(n.)*	critic *(n.)* 🔑
appealing *(adj.)*	deceptive *(adj.)*
appear *(v.)* 🔑	figure out *(phr. v.)*
claim *(v.)* 🔑	hire *(v.)* 🔑
come close to *(phr. v.)*	particularly *(adv.)* 🔑

🔑 Oxford 3000™ words

D. Go online to listen and practice your pronunciation.

WORK WITH THE READING

)) **A.** Read the article and gather information about whether advertising helps or harms us.

Food Advertising Tricks You Should Know About

1   Has this ever happened to you? You're walking down a city street and it's lunchtime. You see an advertisement on a bus showing a beautiful-looking burger. Suddenly, you're starving. Now you know exactly what you want to eat for lunch. You find the nearest fast-food restaurant and order your burger, as your stomach grumbles in **anticipation**. And then you get the food. It doesn't look anything like the picture that you saw in the ad. Why is that?

2   Many food businesses, such as restaurants and food companies, **hire** someone called a "food stylist" to help photograph the foods that they sell. And the reason the "real" food might look different is because the food stylist uses "tricks" to make the food look better, and many of the things they use are not even edible.

3   Take a simple burger as an example. To get the perfect-looking burger, food stylists often will use a partially cooked burger patty because it will **appear** plumper. But how do they get that just-cooked look? Well, a useful tool is a small blowtorch[1], which can burn marks into the burger to make it look like it was grilled. Brown food coloring and some oil are then painted onto the burger to make it look yummy. Now it's time to **figure out** how to photograph the bun. Photographers might need hundreds of buns before they can find the "perfect" bun. And if it's a sesame bun, they'll need a pair of tweezers[2] to glue on the sesame seeds in just the right spot. Often the bun is held in place with toothpicks, so it won't move, and paper towels are placed under the burger so that it doesn't drip all over the bun and make it soggy. Finally, a perfect piece of lettuce, without any holes or brown spots, is chosen and sprayed with glycerin[3] and water, so that it looks fresh. The same is done to the perfect slice of tomato. Sound appetizing?

4   The same sort of **deceptive** tricks are used to photograph turkeys. When a turkey is cooked, it gets wrinkles and the skin does not always look very **appealing**. So the photographer cooks it only part-way, so the skin doesn't wrinkle. To make the skin look very tight, it is sewn with needle and thread underneath. Then the bird can be painted with red and brown food coloring or molasses to give it that "cooked" look. Finally, that handy tool, the blowtorch, is used to make the skin and legs look brown as if it had just come out of the oven.

5   Food stylists use these and many other tricks to make foods look more appealing, but is this deceptive? In the U.S. there is a law that if a company is advertising a food, the real food must be used in the photograph. But since many real foods do not look that good, photo stylists can add other items and use various tools to make foods appear better than they actually look. For example, if an ad is selling chocolate syrup, the other foods in the picture do not have to be real. Fake ice cream is used for such an ad. Using

---

[1] **blowtorch:** a portable device producing a hot flame that is directed onto a surface

[2] **tweezers:** a small tool consisting of two pieces of metal that are joined at one end; used for picking up small things

[3] **glycerin:** a syrupy, sweet liquid made from oil

ingredients like corn syrup, powdered sugar and margarine, fake ice cream looks, but certainly doesn't taste, like the real thing. But it's good for the photographer because it doesn't melt!

6   There are **critics** of this type of practice. They **claim** that advertising companies are deceiving us. They feel that it is unfair to consumers and the law should be changed so photographers will not be allowed to use toothpicks and glue on food they are photographing. They argue that some foods, which may not be **particularly** healthy for consumers, appear appetizing in these "styled" photos because the greasy, unhealthy side is unseen. Perhaps consumers would not be so

quick to run out and grab that burger and fries if the photos showed them as they actually are. But photographers and advertisers disagree. They believe that consumers want to see food at its best, and they feel that it is their job to make the food look good. When food is put under hot lights for hours, it starts to look terrible. Who would want to eat something that doesn't look good?

7   So the next time you see an ad for a mouth-watering burger or roasted turkey, don't be surprised when the real thing doesn't **come close to** looking like the picture in the ad. At least the real thing doesn't come with the glue and toothpicks.

Vocabulary
Skill Review

In Unit 2, you learned how to find the meaning of words from the context. Be sure to use context clues to help you choose the correct words in Activity B.

B. VOCABULARY Complete each sentence with the vocabulary from Reading 1.

anticipation *(n.)*	**critic** *(n.)*
appealing *(adj.)*	**deceptive** *(adj.)*
appear *(v.)*	**figure out** *(phr. v.)*
claim *(v.)*	**hire** *(v.)*
come close to *(phr. v)*	**particularly** *(adv.)*

1. The young child was very hungry, so the pictures of the food items on the menu all looked _____ to him.

2. I need to lose weight, but I hate eating low-fat foods; the taste of low-fat foods doesn't _____ the taste of the real foods.

3. Sometimes the _____ of something happening is better than when it actually happens.

4. The company is doing very well, and they hope to _____ ten new employees by the end of the year.

5. Almost everyone at the meeting agreed with the town's decision, but there was one _____ who argued that it was the wrong choice.

6. Food photographers _____ that it is impossible to take attractive photos of real foods like ice cream.

7. Sam is going away for his vacation, but he still needs to _____ the cheapest way to travel, since he does not have a lot of money to spend.

8. The store advertisement was very _____ because it wasn't clear that you had to spend more than $200 to get the free DVD.

9. I wasn't _____ interested in seeing the movie, but I was pleasantly surprised at how exciting it really was.

10. Toys don't always _____ like they are pictured in ads; often they are much smaller and not as colorful.

iQ ONLINE **C.** Go online for more practice with the vocabulary.

D. Read the main ideas. Write the paragraph number where they are found.

____ 1. There are many tricks for making a burger look good in a photograph.

____ 2. A food stylist might work for a restaurant to take pictures of foods that make them look appetizing.

____ 3. Sometimes the pictures of foods in an advertisement look very different from the real foods.

____ 4. According to the law, photos that food stylists help with are not deceptive as long as the food being advertised is the real food.

____ 5. Taking a picture of a turkey involves using many tricks.

E. Read the statements. Write *T* (true) or *F* (false). Then correct each false statement to make it true according to the article.

____ 1. According to the law, photos from fast-food restaurants must always look just like what you order.

____ 2. A food company hires a food stylist to make its products look more appealing.

____ 3. Food stylists use paint and glue to make photos of food look better.

____ 4. It is not difficult to take photos of a cooked turkey.

____ 5. Food stylists make sure that burgers and turkeys are cooked completely before they photograph them.

F. The article discusses many tricks that are used to make food look more appealing. Complete the chart below with the solution or trick from the box to solve the problem.

Use paper towels.	~~Use a blowtorch for grill marks.~~
Sew it with needle and thread.	Use ingredients like corn syrup and sugar.
Only cook it part-way.	Paint it with food coloring or molasses.

Problem	Solution or trick
1. Cooked burger doesn't look plump.	
2. Partially cooked burger doesn't look cooked.	Use a blowtorch for grill marks.
3. Burger is dripping grease.	
4. Turkey has very loose skin.	
5. Turkey doesn't look cooked.	
6. Ice cream melts under hot lights.	

G. In Activity F, you identified solutions or tricks to make food look better in advertising. Discuss with a partner how these tricks work. Look back at the article for details.

H. Find these sentences in Reading 1. Circle the answer that best matches the meaning of the underlined words. Are there any words from Reading 1 that helped you figure out the meanings? Write them on the lines.

1. (Paragraph 1) You find the nearest fast-food restaurant and order your burger, as your stomach <u>grumbles</u> in anticipation.

   grumbles means
   a. complains
   b. makes a sound when you're hungry
   c. waits

   Words that helped me: <u>You see . . . a beautiful-looking burger. . . . Suddenly,</u>

   <u>you're starving.</u>

2. (Paragraph 2) . . . the food stylist uses "tricks" to make the food look better, and many of the things they use are not even <u>edible</u>.

    edible means   a. good or safe to eat

                                   b. fresh

                                   c. available

    Words that helped me: _____

    _____

3. (Paragraph 5) <u>Fake</u> ice cream is used for such an ad.

    fake means   a. genuine

                                   b. not real

                                   c. actual

    Words that helped me: _____

    _____

I. An inference is a guess you make about something based on the information you have. Make inferences to answer these questions. Write the paragraph number where you found the information. Discuss your answers with a partner.

1. Why do you think photographers might need hundreds of buns before they take a picture of one? Paragraph: ____

2. What might happen if a photographer had to take a picture of frozen yogurt? Paragraph: ____

3. What might happen if a photographer had to take a picture of real French fries on a plate? Paragraph: ____

J. Go online to read *Concerns with Online Advertising* and check your comprehension.

WRITE WHAT YOU THINK

A. Discuss these questions in a group.

1. Food stylists believe that they are helping the food company sell food by making it look appealing, but others think that this is deceptive advertising. What do you think?

2. Would you buy a particular food if the picture of it was not appealing? Why or why not? Is it important to you that food looks appetizing?

3. Have you ever ordered something from a catalog and found that the real item looked very different from the picture in the catalog? How was it different?

B. **Choose one question and write a paragraph in response. Look back at your Quick Write on page 83 as you think about what you learned.**

Reading Skill	Distinguishing facts from opinions

A **fact** is a statement that is true and can be proven true. An **opinion** usually expresses a personal judgment or gives a position about something. Good readers can quickly tell whether a statement is a fact or an opinion. Look at these two statements.

> My parents have been married for 25 years. (fact)
> Relationships with human beings are messy and unpredictable. (opinion)

The first statement is a fact. We can find the date of their marriage and prove it. The second statement is an opinion. It cannot be proven, and people could have a different opinion about relationships from the writer's. In addition, adjectives such as *messy* and *unpredictable* indicate the writer's opinion. Here are two more examples.

> Class starts at 7:30 a.m. (fact)
> My classes are difficult. (opinion)

A. Read the statements. Write *F* (fact) or *O* (opinion).

____ 1. Some ads try to make people aware of social problems.

____ 2. There were eight ads for appliances in a recent news magazine.

____ 3. Advertising can be ignored easily.

____ 4. During every half-hour television show, there are 12 minutes of commercial advertising.

____ 5. The ads during the sports program were very funny.

____ 6. Ads create a dangerous climate of distrust.

B. Read the sentences. Underline the part of each sentence that makes it an opinion.

1. People are always influenced by ads.

2. Taken individually, ads are silly, sometimes funny, but certainly nothing to worry about.

3. My favorite ad is the one showing the family in the beautiful new car.

4. That was the most ridiculous ad I have ever seen.

5. The consequences of ads are harmful.

 **C.** Go online for more practice distinguishing facts from opinions.

READING 2 | In Defense of Advertising

 You are going to read an article based on a Canadian radio show. It gives us a less common opinion of advertising. Use the article to gather information and ideas for your Unit Assignment.

PREVIEW THE READING

A. PREVIEW Read the title and first sentence of each paragraph. Do you think the writer finds advertising to be positive or negative? Check (✓) your answer.

☐ positive   ☐ negative

B. QUICK WRITE Think about an advertisement that provided useful information about something important to you. Write for 5–10 minutes in response. Be sure to use this section for your Unit Assignment.

C. VOCABULARY Work with a partner to find the words in the reading. Circle clues in the text that help you understand the meaning of each word. Then use a dictionary to define any unknown words.

annoying *(adj.)* 🔑	donation *(n.)*	memorable *(adj.)*
annual *(adj.)* 🔑	entertain *(v.)* 🔑	support *(v.)* 🔑
broadcasting *(n.)*	exposure *(n.)*	surrounding *(adj.)* 🔑

🔑 Oxford 3000™ words

 **D.** Go online to listen and practice your pronunciation.

WORK WITH THE READING

A. Read the article and gather information about whether advertising helps or harms us.

In Defense of Advertising

1   How often do we hear comments such as these: "I hate advertising," or "There's too much advertising in the world!" In the 21st century, it seems that advertising is everywhere we look. We see it along highways, in trains, buses, even in taxicabs, as well as on the Internet and on TV. It's hard to escape advertising. But do we really want to? Actually, when you think about it, advertising provides us with quite a few benefits.

2   First, advertising gives us information that we need. For instance, if you want to buy a new appliance or a new car, you can look for the best "deals" in ads that appear in newspapers, in magazines, on television, or even on the radio. These ads give you details about the product and help you find out where you can get the best price for something. You don't actually have to go to lots of different stores. So, in this way, advertising provides a service for the consumer.

3   Besides providing information, advertising also **supports** the entertainment industry, including television and radio. It may be **annoying** to sit through commercials during your favorite TV show, but the advertisers have paid for its production. This, in turn, pays the TV crew for their work. Even public **broadcasting** has supporters. The companies' names appear at the beginning or end of the shows. Without their support, there would be more hours of pledge drives[1] asking you, the consumer, for more money. Many presenters, such as newsreaders, get their starts from writing or appearing in commercials or print advertisements. It's a way for them to get both experience and **exposure**.

4   And what about advertising and sports? There are hundreds of large banners **surrounding** sports stadiums, and hundreds, thousands, even millions of people notice them. Professional sports depend on advertising to pay for the fields, the equipment, and yes, even the salaries of professional athletes. Think about the Super Bowl in the United States. Everyone looks forward to this **annual** event, even those who do not like football, because the commercials are known to be the best of the year. Companies pay as much as a million dollars for 60 seconds of advertising time during this event, so a lot of effort goes into these

[1] **pledge drive:** an effort by a group of people to raise money, which people promise to pay, for a certain purpose or group

commercials. As a result, viewers want to watch the commercials almost as much as the sports.

5   When we're not out shopping or being **entertained**, many of us enjoy surfing the Web. Whenever you open a page in Google or access an online newspaper, such as the *New York Times*, there are dozens of ads. These ads help pay for the services that the websites provide. Without the advertising, the websites could not provide those services. They would not have the money to continue.

6   There has always been a "good" side to advertising in the form of public service announcements (PSAs). These are advertisements that provide people with information about issues like diseases or medical problems, as well as public health and safety. The commercials are often very creative and informative. They provide viewers with the information they need in a **memorable** way. Various companies pay for the PSAs, and advertising agencies make **donations** of their time and expertise to produce them.

7   It would be a much duller, certainly less colorful world without advertising. Think of all of the ways that advertising improves our world. The next time you look at that clothing catalog, think of all of the creativity and work that went into making it. From clothing designers and photographers to paper company workers and store employees—thousands of people worked to help produce that catalog. And when you watch your favorite TV show, remember that the commercials were partly responsible for what you've just watched and enjoyed. We may wish that commercials and advertisements weren't necessary, but, for the most part, we are all content to have them as part of our lives.

Vocabulary Skill Review

Knowing the part of speech of a vocabulary word can help you understand the text better. Use the context to guess the part of speech of the words in Activity B.

B. VOCABULARY Here are some words from Reading 2. Read the sentences. Then write each bold word next to the correct definition on page 93.

1. Some food companies use part of their profits to **support** programs for seriously ill children.

2. This is a useful website, but I can't stand all of the pop-up ads. They're so **annoying**!

3. Radio **broadcasting** brings news and other programs to the public.

4. The professor's appearance on the news program gave him the **exposure** he needed to become well known.

5. All of the ads on the fence **surrounding** the baseball field are for food products that are sold there.

6. There is always a guest speaker at the college's **annual** graduation dinner. This year, it will be the mayor!

7. The children were bored last night, so we turned on the TV to **entertain** them.

8. That was a very **memorable** book. After all these years, I still remember the ending very clearly.

9. Many food companies make a **donation** of their products to organizations that feed the hungry.

a. _____ (*adj.*) being or going around someone or something

b. _____ (*v.*) to interest and amuse someone

c. _____ (*n.*) attention from newspapers, television, or other media

d. _____ (*n.*) sound or pictures that are sent by radio or television

e. _____ (*n.*) money or something that is given to an organization

f. _____ (*adj.*) happening or done once a year

g. _____ (*v.*) to give or provide someone or something with assistance and money

h. _____ (*adj.*) making you feel slightly angry

i. _____ (*adj.*) easy to remember because it is special in some way

iQ ONLINE   **C.** Go online for more practice with the vocabulary.

D. Read the sentences. Then number them in the order that the ideas appear in the article.

____ a. PSAs provide people with information about things like medical problems.

____ b. Professional sports depend on advertising.

____ c. Advertising helps support broadcasting.

____ d. Ads provide us with helpful information about products we want to buy.

____ e. Advertisements make the world more colorful.

____ f. Ads help pay for the services that websites provide.

E. Write an example for each of the benefits of advertising listed in the chart.

Benefit	Example
provides information for buying something	best deal for new car in newspaper
supports broadcasting	
helps support sports	
provides public service announcements	
helps make the world more colorful	

F. Read the statements. Write *A* if the author would agree with a statement, or *D* if the author would disagree with it. Write the paragraph number(s) to support your answer.

	Agree/ Disagree	Paragraph #
1. There are more advantages than disadvantages to advertising.	A	1, 7
2. Many newsreaders gained experience by doing commercials.		
3. Most people enjoy watching commercials during their favorite shows.		
4. Professional sports fields should not have advertising.		
5. We should have less advertising and more fundraising on TV.		

G. Answer the questions. Write the paragraph number where the answer is found. Then discuss your answers with a partner.

1. In professional sports, what are some examples of things that advertising pays for?

   Paragraph: ____

2. What kinds of professionals work on a clothing catalog? Name at least three.

Paragraph: _____

_____

3. Why is it important that PSAs be very creative?

Paragraph: _____

_____

4. What would not exist on the Internet if there were no advertising?

Paragraph: _____

_____

WRITE WHAT YOU THINK

A. Discuss the questions in a group. Look back at your Quick Write on page 90 as you think about what you learned.

1. Some people say that advertising is a "necessary evil." What does this mean? Do you agree? Why or why not? (If something is *evil*, it is very bad.)

2. Would you be willing to pay more for things and have no advertising?

B. Before you watch the video, discuss the questions in a group.

1. Where can you find advertising that targets children? What kinds of ads can they be?

2. What effects do you think advertising can have on children?

C. Go online to watch the video about advertising to children. Then check your comprehension.

> **cope with** *(phr. v.)* to deal successfully with a difficult matter or situation
>
> **emblematic** *(adj.)* represents or is a symbol of something
>
> **hypocritical** *(adj.)* someone who pretends to have moral beliefs that they do not really have
>
> **regulate** *(v.)* to control something by using laws

VIDEO VOCABULARY

D. Think about the unit video, Reading 1, and Reading 2 as you discuss the questions. Then choose one question and write a paragraph in response.

1. Think of an advertisement that you've seen recently that affected you. What was it selling? How did it affect you? Was it positive or negative?

2. Do you think there is too much advertising? Where would you like to see less or no advertising?

3. Do you think advertising to children is harmful? Do you think it should be regulated? Why or why not?

| Vocabulary Skill | Suffixes |

A **suffix** is a group of letters that comes at the end of a word, such as *-ful* in *painful*. When you add a suffix to a word, it changes the part of speech. Being familiar with suffixes can help increase your vocabulary. Here is a list of suffixes.

Adjective		Noun		Adverb
-ful	-ial	-ment	-ship	-ly
-able	-er	-tion	-ness	

Tip for Success

Being familiar with suffixes used to form nouns and adjectives will help you in your writing and in your reading comprehension.

A. Decide which part of speech each word is based on its suffix. Then check (✓) the correct column.

	Adjective	Noun	Adverb
1. unpredictable	☐	☐	☐
2. relationship	☐	☐	☐
3. recently	☐	☐	☐
4. painful	☐	☐	☐
5. dissatisfaction	☐	☐	☐
6. distrustful	☐	☐	☐
7. happiness	☐	☐	☐
8. donation	☐	☐	☐
9. certainly	☐	☐	☐
10. colorful	☐	☐	☐

 B. Go online for more practice with suffixes.

WRITING

UNIT OBJECTIVE ▶▶▶ At the end of this unit, you will write an opinion essay about advertising. This essay will include specific information from the readings and your own ideas.

Writing Skill | Writing an opinion essay

In Unit 1, you learned the components, or parts, of a good paragraph. An **essay** is a longer piece of writing, and it has components similar to the ones in a paragraph. In an essay, the first paragraph is the **introductory paragraph**. In an **opinion essay**, the introductory paragraph describes a situation and includes your opinion of it, which is the main idea of the essay. In an essay, this main idea is called a **thesis statement**. The thesis statement of an opinion essay clearly expresses how you feel about the topic.

The next paragraphs in an essay are the **body paragraphs**. The body paragraphs support the thesis statement. In an opinion essay, a body paragraph gives a specific reason for your opinion and examples to make it a strong argument. Finally, the **concluding paragraph** is the last paragraph. It restates your opinion, summarizes your reasons for it, and often gives a prediction about it.

A. **WRITING MODEL** Read the model opinion essay. Then answer the questions on page 98.

Introductory paragraph

Most people love watching some kind of television, but hate the commercials that interrupt the TV programs. I guess you could say that I'm different from most people because I love commercials. In fact, I think the commercials are almost as good as the shows I'm watching. You won't find me leaving the room to get a snack or something to drink when a commercial comes on. I'm the one paying attention because I think television commercials are great!

Body paragraph

First of all, I think a lot of commercials are funny. Some advertisers like to make fun of mistakes that people make. For example, a car insurance company has an ad showing a man trimming a tree in his yard. The next thing you know, a huge tree limb falls on his neighbor's car. It's what they used to call slapstick humor, and I think it's very funny. In another example, some guys are moving into a new apartment and they are installing an air conditioner into a window, and it falls out and onto someone's car. I enjoy these kinds of commercials because they provide a glimpse of human behavior that I find entertaining.

Body paragraphs

Additionally, I like to see commercials that my senses respond to, in particular my sense of taste. When I see a close-up of some mouth-watering food, I get so hungry that I have to eat it. I frequently call for takeout right then and there, or I run to the kitchen and try to create what I've just seen on the screen. When I see a new car ad where the car is driving through mountain roads, it makes me want to book a trip out west to enjoy the same scenery. And when I hear music I like as the background to one of my programs, I make sure to pay attention to the credits at the end to find out the name of the musician so I can listen to that person again.

Finally, TV advertising provides me with information about coming attractions: future TV programs, events, or movies. When I see a commercial for a movie that will soon be released, I can decide if it's something I want to see or not. If there's a TV program coming up, I can set my DVR for it well in advance.

Concluding paragraph

You could say I'm very unusual because I don't mind commercials while I'm watching my favorite TV programs. I don't find commercials to be interruptions. I love them because I think they're funny, entertaining, and informative. I think TV would be pretty dull without them.

1. What is the thesis statement? Underline the thesis statement in the introductory paragraph.

2. What are the three reasons and examples that the writer uses to support his or her opinion?

Reason 1: I think a lot of commercials are funny.

Examples: A huge tree limb falls on a neighbor's car; an air conditioner falls out a window and onto someone's car.

Reason 2: _____

Examples: _____

_____

Reason 3: _____

Examples: _____

_____

B. Read these introductory paragraphs to different opinion essays. Which is the best thesis statement for each essay? Choose from the statements below.

1. Advertising has been around for many years, and most people just accept it as part of our lives. But I was watching TV with my young son the other night when he pointed out to me the name of a particular computer

Writing Tip

The thesis statement of an essay is similar to the topic sentence of a paragraph. It contains the writer's main idea, position, or opinion. It helps the reader understand the writer's main idea.

that he noticed on the show we were watching. That's when I realized that advertising has invaded our lives too much. If my son recognizes a company logo that easily, I wonder how much more advertising he is being exposed to without even realizing it? Enough is enough.

a. There should not be any advertising on the Internet.

b. Advertising products within television shows should be banned.

c. We need to find a way to reduce the amount of advertising in our lives.

2. While watching my son's baseball game the other night, I noticed something new on the fence surrounding the field. There was a huge advertisement for a popular brand of soda. I was absolutely shocked! How could an advertisement for junk food be placed in view of all of the children and parents? I realize now that this huge corporation is giving money to my son's school, but at what cost?

a. Advertisements for unhealthy food or drinks should not be on school property.

b. I think soda advertisements are very funny.

c. I think it's wonderful that companies are paying for sports programs.

3. With new technology, advertising can be very deceptive. For example, many beauty ads show women with perfect skin and hair. In reality, their photos have been "touched up" by computer software programs. Men, too, are shown as very muscular and strong, when the reality may be quite different. Men and women both age naturally, but advertisements show a different kind of person—one who never gets old.

a. I think changing the way someone looks in a photo is an outdated advertising trick.

b. I think advertisements should show people of different ages, shapes, and sizes, not just young people.

c. I think computer software programs are very innovative.

4. I was watching TV last night and I realized something about my life: I'm missing a lot of things. When I saw a commercial for a new sports car, I realized I don't have the most modern car. An ad for flat-screen TVs reminded me that my television is eight years old. And finally, the travel commercials reminded me that I don't have the money to travel to exotic places and stay in world-famous resorts. So, in the end, all of these ads make me feel like a failure. This is not a reason why I watch TV.

a. Advertising on TV should provide us with details about all the latest products.

b. Advertising on TV should entertain us.

c. Advertising on TV should not make us feel like we are unsuccessful.

 C. Go online for more practice with writing an opinion essay.

A **simple sentence** contains a *subject* and a *verb* and expresses a complete thought or idea. A simple sentence is sometimes called an *independent clause*.

Ahmed drives to work every day.
   subject   verb

A **compound sentence** contains two **independent clauses** (or simple sentences) joined by a **coordinating conjunction** (*and*, *but*, *so*, *or*). A comma usually comes before the coordinating conjunction in a compound sentence.

Use *and* to combine two sentences with related ideas.

The ad was funny, **and** it gave us helpful information.

Use *but* to combine two sentences with contrasting ideas.

I enjoyed the book, **but** it had a very sad ending.

Use *so* when the second sentence is a result of the first sentence.

Ali isn't feeling well, **so** he isn't coming to class today.

Use *or* when there is a choice or two possibilities.

You can take the train to Madrid, **or** you can fly.

Using different types of sentences can help make your writing more interesting for your reader.

A. Complete each sentence with *and*, *or*, *but*, or *so*. Then write the reason you chose that conjunction (*related ideas*, *a choice*, *contrasting ideas*, or *a result*).

1. I am the mother of young children, ___and___ I feel that all advertising during children's programming should be banned.

   Reason: _____ related ideas _____

2. The TV advertisement was about a very serious social topic, _____ there were some funny moments in it.

   Reason: _____

3. Children are exposed to many advertisements for unhealthy foods, _____ parents have to educate their children about good food and nutrition.

   Reason: _____

4. Many people think advertisements are harmful, _____ sometimes they can be very helpful.

Reason: _____

5. We can use a Web ad, _____ we can create a TV ad.

Reason: _____

B. Combine the sentences with *and, or, but,* or *so*. Add commas.

1. I like to stay healthy. I exercise every day.

_____

2. Sara Marcone is a very creative writer. She has written five novels.

_____

3. The lecture was interesting. It was a bit too long.

_____

4. We can go out for dinner. We can stay home.

_____

C. Write five compound sentences. Use each conjunction (*and, or, but, so*) at least once.

D. Find five compound sentences in Reading 2 on pages 91–92. Underline the sentences and circle the coordinating conjunctions.

E. Go online for more practice with compound sentences.

F. Go online for the grammar expansion.

| Unit Assignment | Write an opinion essay |

In this assignment, you are going to write a four-paragraph opinion essay about advertising. As you prepare your essay, think about the Unit Question, "Does advertising help or harm us?" Use information from Reading 1, Reading 2, the unit video, and your work in this unit to support your essay. Refer to the Self-Assessment checklist on page 102.

Go to the Online Writing Tutor for a writing model and alternate Unit Assignments.

PLAN AND WRITE

A. BRAINSTORM Think about your answer to the Unit Question, "Does advertising help or harm us?" Then write a list of reasons and examples for your answer or opinion.

B. PLAN Follow these steps to plan your opinion essay.

1. Read your list from Activity A. Circle your best reasons and examples.

2. Write your thesis statement below. It should tell the reader your opinion about the topic.

_____

3. Go to the Online Resources to download and complete the outline for your opinion essay.

C. WRITE Use your PLAN notes to write your essay. Go to *iQ Online* to use the Online Writing Tutor.

1. Write your opinion essay. Remember to state your opinion in the introductory paragraph. Include at least two reasons for your opinion in the two body paragraphs.

2. Look at the Self-Assessment checklist below to guide your writing.

REVISE AND EDIT

A. PEER REVIEW Read your partner's essay. Then go online and use the Peer Review worksheet. Discuss the review with your partner.

B. REWRITE Based on your partner's review, revise and rewrite your essay.

C. EDIT Complete the Self-Assessment checklist as you prepare to write the final draft of your opinion essay. Be prepared to hand in your work or discuss it in class.

SELF-ASSESSMENT		
Yes	No	
☐	☐	Does the essay include an introductory paragraph, two body paragraphs, and a concluding paragraph?
☐	☐	Are compound sentences used appropriately?
☐	☐	If words with suffixes are used, are they correct?
☐	☐	Does the essay include vocabulary from the unit?
☐	☐	Did you check the essay for punctuation, spelling, and grammar?

 **D. REFLECT** Go to the Online Discussion Board to discuss these questions.

1. What is something new you learned in this unit?

2. Look back at the Unit Question—Does advertising help or harm us? Is your answer different now than when you started the unit? If yes, how is it different? Why?

TRACK YOUR SUCCESS

Circle the words and phrases you have learned in this unit.

Nouns
anticipation AWL
broadcasting
critic 🔑
dissatisfaction
donation
exposure
happiness 🔑
relationship 🔑

Verbs
appear 🔑
claim 🔑
entertain 🔑
hire 🔑
support 🔑

Phrasal Verbs
come close to
figure out

Adjectives
annoying 🔑
annual 🔑 AWL
appealing
colorful
deceptive
distrustful
memorable
painful 🔑
surrounding 🔑

Adverbs
certainly 🔑
messy 🔑
particularly 🔑
recently 🔑
unpredictable AWL

🔑 Oxford 3000™ words
AWL Academic Word List

Check (✓) the skills you learned. If you need more work on a skill, refer to the page(s) in parentheses.

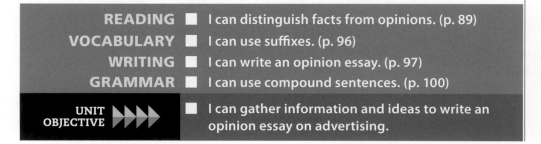

READING ☐ I can distinguish facts from opinions. (p. 89)
VOCABULARY ☐ I can use suffixes. (p. 96)
WRITING ☐ I can write an opinion essay. (p. 97)
GRAMMAR ☐ I can use compound sentences. (p. 100)

UNIT OBJECTIVE ▶▶▶ ☐ I can gather information and ideas to write an opinion essay on advertising.

READING ▶ using referents to understand contrast
VOCABULARY ▶ using the dictionary to find the correct meaning
WRITING ▶ writing a narrative essay
GRAMMAR ▶ shifts between past and present time frames

UNIT QUESTION

Why do people take risks?

A Discuss these questions with your classmates.

1. What does "take a risk" mean?

2. Are you a risk-taker? If so, what kinds of risks do you take?

3. Look at the photos. What are the people doing? Did you ever do any of these activities? Do you want to? Why or why not?

UNIT ►►►► Read the article and book excerpt and gather information
OBJECTIVE and ideas to write a narrative essay about a risk you
have taken.

🔊 **B** Listen to *The Q Classroom* online. Then answer
these questions.

1. Marcus thinks that some people take risks for the
   excitement. Do you think that's a common reason
   for people to take risks? What kinds of risks bring
   someone excitement?

2. Sophy and Felix talk about a different kind of risk,
   one that involves doing something new, like starting
   a new job, or moving to a new place. Do you feel that
   these things are also risky? How are they risky?
   Did you ever take a risk like this?

iQ ONLINE **C** Go online to watch the video about taking risks.
Then check your comprehension.

arduous *(adj.)* involving a lot of effort
and energy

confines *(n.)* limits or borders

margin for error *(phr. n.)* room to make
a mistake

mundane *(adj.)* not interesting or
exciting

scaling *(v.)* climbing to the top of
something

spectacular *(adj.)* very impressive

VIDEO VOCABULARY

iQ ONLINE **D** Go to the Online Discussion Board to discuss
the Unit Question with your classmates.

105

PREVIEW THE UNIT

E Look at the photos. Number them in order of risk. Use 1 for the riskiest and 6 for the least risky. Then compare your answers with a partner and discuss why you made your choices.

____ skiing   ____ mountain climbing   ____ rock climbing

____ motocross   ____ whitewater rafting   ____ bungee jumping

F Look at the photos. Which job do you think is the most dangerous? Number them from 1 to 6. Use 1 for the most dangerous. Then compare your answers with your partner and discuss why you made your choices.

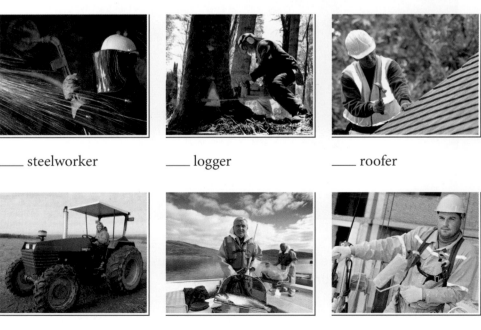

____ steelworker   ____ logger   ____ roofer

____ farmer   ____ fisherman   ____ painter

READING

READING 1 | Fear Factor: Success and Risk in Extreme Sports

You are going to read an article from *National Geographic News* that looks at why some people do extreme sports. Extreme sports are sports that most people think are very risky. Use the article to gather information and ideas for your Unit Assignment.

PREVIEW THE READING

A. PREVIEW Read the first sentence of each paragaph. Why do you think people do things like extreme sports? Check (✓) your ideas.

☐ They don't think it's too risky.

☐ They secretly want to get hurt.

☐ They like a challenge.

☐ They love the feeling of excitement.

☐ It makes them focus on the present moment.

☐ They want to be famous.

☐ Other reasons _____

_____

B. QUICK WRITE Think about a sport or an activity that is very risky. Write for 5–10 minutes in response. Be sure to use this section for your Unit Assignment.

C. VOCABULARY Check (✓) the words you know. Then work with a partner to locate each word in the reading. Use clues to help define the words you don't know. Check your definitions in the dictionary.

aspect *(n.)* 🔑	perceive *(v.)*	tolerance *(n.)*
challenge *(n.)* 🔑	precaution *(n.)*	trait *(n.)*
mental *(adj.)* 🔑	pursuit *(n.)*	vivid *(adj.)*
notable *(adj.)*		

🔑 Oxford 3000™ words

 **D.** Go online to listen and practice your pronunciation.

WORK WITH THE READING

» **A. Read the article and gather information about why people take risks.**

Fear Factor: Success and Risk in Extreme Sports

1   Every year in Pamplona, Spain, hundreds of people run alongside 1,300-pound (600-kilo) bulls, just for the fun of it. And every year at least a few of these people are injured, some seriously. Yet this does not stop people from participating in the event.

2   What is it that drives some people to embrace extreme risks, while the rest of us run to the safety of the sidelines[1]? Lester Keller, a longtime coach and sports-psychology coordinator for the U.S. Ski and Snowboard Association, says that not everyone has the **mental** character to excel in dangerous **pursuits**. He notes that most of us reach a point that limits our appetite for extreme risk and, as a result, our ability to perform well in dangerous conditions. But others have a much higher **tolerance** for risk. Take the example of Daron Rahlves, a top U.S. downhill ski racer. "The high element of risk makes you feel alive, tests what you are made of and how far you can take yourself," Rahlves said in a previous interview with U.S. Ski Team staff. "I'm not looking for danger. I'm in it for the **challenge**, my heart thumping as I finish, the feeling of being alive," he said. "I definitely get scared on some of the courses. It just makes me fight more. . . . That's when I do best."

3   The fear that drives many people away from the risks of extreme sports may be the same ingredient that keeps others coming back for more. Mountaineer Al Read has logged many **notable** first ascents[2] over the course of his climbing career. Having climbed for over 40 years, Read says he no longer pushes to the extremes as he once did—but the feeling is still **vivid**. "I can remember when I was getting into situations where I thought that at any moment I could be killed," he told *National Geographic News*. ". . . I would say, '. . . I'll never do this again.' But we'd get back down, and when we were safe we'd say, 'Man was that great!'" he recalled. "You forget how scary it was, and you go back again."

4   In addition to not being afraid of risks, certain people may **perceive** risk differently from others. Shane Murphy, a sports psychologist and professor at Western Connecticut State University, has worked with Olympians and other athletes. He says he is struck by the way they redefine risk according to their skills, experience, and environment. He worked with a group climbing Everest without oxygen, which to him was the riskiest thing anyone could do. But the climbers took every **precaution** to prepare themselves for this climb. As Murphy describes it, "To them it was the next step in an activity that they've done

---

[1] **sidelines:** the lines that form the edges of a sports field

[2] **ascent:** a climb to the top of a mountain

for years. They weren't going out there to get hurt." Murphy said the perspective of extreme athletes is very different from our own. "We look at a risky situation and know that if we were in that situation, we would be out of control," he said. "But from the athletes' perspective, they have a lot of control, and there are a lot of things that they do to minimize risk." Statistically, mountain climbing is not as risky as people think it is. Our perceived risk of the sport leaves the majority of us at the bottom of the mountain.

5 Another key **aspect** of risk perception may be something referred to as "the flow" or "the zone." It is a state in which many athletes describe becoming absorbed in pursuits that focus the mind completely on the present. "Something that makes you begin climbing, perhaps, is that your adrenaline flows and you become very concentrated on what you're doing," Read said. "After it's over there's exhilaration[3]. You wouldn't have that same feeling if the risk hadn't been there." Psychologists note that some people seem to have a strong craving for adrenaline rushes[4] as a thrill-seeking behavior or personality **trait**. As a result, these types of people may always be driven to adventures that others consider extreme. "I can enjoy hitting the tennis ball around, because that's my skill level," Murphy said. "But others might need the challenge of Olympic competition."

[3] **exhilaration:** a feeling of being very happy and alive
[4] **adrenaline rush:** a feeling of being very excited and happy, brought about from the body chemical of the same name

B. VOCABULARY Here are some words from Reading 1. Read the sentences. Circle the answer that best matches the meaning of each bold word. Then compare your answers with a partner.

1. Running a marathon requires both physical strength and strong **mental** qualities like confidence and determination.
   a. relating to the mind
   b. relating to the body

2. Joe Simpson is **notable** for his mountain climbing as well as his writing.
   a. intelligent
   b. important and well known

3. In order to really enjoy skiing, you need to have a very high **tolerance** for the cold.
   a. ability to accept something difficult or unpleasant
   b. knowledge about a subject

4. During the summer months, some of his athletic **pursuits** are running, biking, and mountain climbing.
   a. activities
   b. teammates

5. He's an experienced climber, and now he believes he's ready for the **challenge** of climbing Mount Everest.
   a. something fun and relaxing
   b. something difficult and exciting

6. My memory of reaching the top of the mountain is so **vivid** that I feel as if I'm still there.
   a. causing pain or discomfort
   b. producing a strong, clear picture in your mind

7. People **perceive** farming as a safe job, but it is one of the riskiest jobs a person can have.
   a. think of
   b. recognize the importance of

8. If you go rock climbing, you should take **precautions**, such as wearing a helmet and the right kind of shoes.
   a. things you do well
   b. things you do to avoid danger

9. One **aspect** of extreme sports that many people cannot overcome is the risk.
   a. part
   b. result

10. One **trait** that extreme sports athletes share is the love of excitement in their sport.
    a. particular quality
    b. problem

 **C.** Go online for more practice with the vocabulary.

Critical Thinking **Tip**

Activity D asks you to locate information in the reading. Locating information in a reading is a useful comprehension activity that helps to confirm that you understand what you have read.

D. Read the main ideas. Write the paragraph number where they are found.

____ 1. Some people may have a stronger desire than others for risks because of the adrenaline flow that they get.

____ 2. Certain people may perceive risk differently from the rest of us.

____ 3. People who enjoy the risks of extreme sports also enjoy the fear.

____ 4. Not everyone has the same tolerance for risk; some of us have a much higher tolerance.

E. Complete the chart. Write an example from Reading 1 for each of the main ideas from Activity D.

Main idea	Example
Higher tolerance of risk	Daron Rahlves, a ski racer
Fear of risk	
Adrenaline flow	
Risk perception	

F. Complete each statement with information from Reading 1.

1. Every year in Pamplona, Spain, hundreds of people run alongside bulls, just for _____.

2. Lester Keller says that not everyone has the _____ to excel in dangerous pursuits.

3. Al Read remembers getting into situations where he thought that at any moment he _____.

4. Shane Murphy worked with a group climbing Mount Everest _____.

5. Statistically, mountain climbing is not as risky as _____.

G. Read the statements below. Choose the person from Reading 1 who might make each statement.

   a. Daron Rahlves

   b. Shane Murphy

   c. Al Read

   d. Lester Keller

1. At the top of the mountain, you tell yourself that you are crazy for doing this, but at the bottom, you feel completely different. ____

2. Many people are happy just playing a game of basketball with their friends. It's very safe and predictable. But other people have a higher tolerance for risk and prefer more high-risk sports. ____

3. Olympic athletes always prepare themselves well for the activity that they are going to do, so they don't perceive it as very risky at all. ____

4. Even though I'm traveling at about 60 miles an hour down a slope, I'm not scared. I'm thrilled. ____

 **H.** Go online to read *The Risks of Farming* and check your comprehension.

WRITE WHAT YOU THINK

A. Discuss these questions in a group.

1. Think of an activity that you think is risky. Why do you think it is risky? Give specific reasons. How would someone who does this activity frequently feel differently about it? Why?

2. Look back at the photos of the jobs on page 106. According to the latest statistics (the number of deaths per 100,000), the most dangerous job pictured is a fisherman. Did you rate fishing as a very dangerous job? Why or why not?

3. Why do you think we perceive activities such as mountain climbing to be riskier than they actually are?

B. Choose one question and write a paragraph in response. Look back at your Quick Write on page 107 as you think about what you learned.

A **referent** is a word or group of words that refers to a noun that was mentioned previously. Understanding referents will help you become a better reader. In Reading 1, the writer is focusing on what makes one group of people (those who enjoy extreme sports) different from everyone else (those who do not enjoy extreme sports). The writer uses certain words and phrases to refer to each group throughout the reading.

Group 1 (the minority)	Group 2 (the majority)
People who enjoy extreme sports	**People who don't enjoy extreme sports**
some people	the rest of us
others	most of us
certain people	many people
they	we
these types of people	

referent: people who don't enjoy extreme sports

He notes that <u>most of us</u> reach a point that limits our appetite for extreme risk....

referent: people who enjoy extreme sports

But <u>others</u> have a much higher tolerance for risk.

A. Read the sentences from Reading 1. Underline the words and phrases that refer to people who enjoy extreme sports. Circle the words and phrases that refer to the majority of people.

1. What is it that drives some people to embrace extreme risks, while the rest of us run to the safety of the sidelines?

2. He notes that most of us reach a point that limits our appetite for extreme risk. . . . But others have a much higher tolerance for risk.

3. The fear that drives many people away from the risks of extreme sports may be the same ingredient that keeps others coming back for more.

4. In addition to not being afraid of risks, certain people may perceive risk differently from others.

5. As a result, these types of people may always be driven to adventures that others consider extreme.

B. Read the paragraph about the types of people who choose to become fishermen. Underline the words and phrases that refer to the fishermen. Circle the words and phrases that refer to the majority of people.

The Life of a Fisherman

What does it take to become a fisherman? It's definitely not for most of us. The majority of people will not want to earn their living on the dangerous seas, working 24 hours, seven days a week, until enough fish are caught. However, some people enjoy the challenge of this type of work. These types of people would not be happy sitting at a desk from nine to five. For them, making a lot of money in a short amount of time is worth the risk. The rest of us would probably prefer our boring lifestyles without the risk. It takes a certain type of person who is willing to be on a boat for three to five months in order to make a living. Perhaps it's the thrill of the unknown that certain types of people look for. The rest of us are content to watch the boats from the safety of the harbor.

 **C.** Go online for more practice using referents to understand contrast.

You are going to read an excerpt from a book called *The Climb of My Life: Scaling Mountains with a Borrowed Heart* by Kelly Perkins. It's about a woman who climbs a mountain ten months after having a heart transplant. A transplant is a type of surgery in which an organ, for example, a heart, liver, or kidney, is replaced. Use the reading to gather information and ideas for your Unit Assignment.

PREVIEW THE READING

A. PREVIEW Read the title and first two paragraphs. Why do you think Kelly took the risk of climbing a mountain?

☐ She wanted to improve her health.

☐ She wanted to improve how she felt about herself.

☐ She likes the excitement of mountain climbing.

B. QUICK WRITE Think about a time when you had a challenge in life, perhaps a physical challenge like an illness. What did you do to help you overcome this challenge? Write for 5–10 minutes in response. Be sure to use this section for your Unit Assignment.

C. VOCABULARY Check (✓) the words you know. Use a dictionary to define any new or unknown words. Then discuss how the words will relate to the unit with a partner.

bravely *(adv.)*	distinctive *(adj.)*	role *(n.)* 🔑
conquer *(v.)*	earn *(v.)* 🔑	significant *(adj.)* 🔑
determined *(adj.)* 🔑	goal *(n.)* 🔑	ultimate *(adj.)* 🔑

🔑 Oxford 3000™ words

 **D.** Go online to listen and practice your pronunciation.

WORK WITH THE READING

A. Read the excerpt from the book and gather information about why people take risks.

THE CLIMB OF MY LIFE

1   *At the age of 30, Kelly Perkins developed a disease of the heart, and after three years of treatment, she received a heart transplant. Ten months later, she climbed to the top of Half Dome Mountain in Yosemite National Park in the United States, and became the first heart transplant patient to do so.*

2   Like life, mountains can be seen as a series of difficulties that you need to overcome. To me, a mountain is the **ultimate** challenge, with body, spirit, and mind all having to work together. Being sick is a challenge, too. Both challenges involve **bravely** facing the unknown, and to **conquer** either requires well-defined **goals** and discipline. Of the two, of course, I'd rather the mountain be my physical challenge than physical challenges be my "mountain."

3   Mountains began to consume my thoughts. Secretly, I wanted to do something **significant** to help change the image that friends and family had developed of me. I had been cast in the **role** of patient. In spite of being very good in that role, I hated being a patient and desperately wanted to change my image. I wanted bruises to be **earned** from sports-related activities, not from needle pricks and aspirin-thinned blood. At this stage, my self-image was as important to my well-being as anything else. If, I figured, I could rebuild my strength and regain at least some of my former athleticism, an improved image would naturally follow.

4   I set a goal—to hike the 4,100-foot ascent of Half Dome in Yosemite. I was drawn to this destination by its beauty, a beauty not because it was perfect, but because it was imperfect. Half Dome's shape is unforgettably **distinctive** because it's broken. If it were whole, it would lose its uniqueness. The spirit-building message wasn't lost on me. Just because I wasn't perfect didn't mean I couldn't stand as tall and mighty as anyone else.

5   In August of 1996, just ten months after my heart replacement, my husband Craig and I began to hike the trail leading to Half Dome. The trail began with a mild incline, which we eagerly took at a brisk pace. I was winded at first, but as soon as my heart caught up with me, I felt energized. I tried to go as fast as the other hikers, but found it difficult to keep up. The canyon had many steep slopes and deep stone stairs, allowing in very

little sunlight, which kept temperatures cool and the rocks slippery.

6   Though the climb's final half-mile isn't technically difficult, the granite dome, angled at 45 degrees, can be extremely intimidating, especially for those afraid of heights. A stairway is used to climb the last 500 feet to the summit. There was a handrail made out of steel cables, connected to stairs made of thin wooden planks. Thrown along the stairs were weathered work gloves, available to help protect the climbers' hands from the "death grip" commonly used during descent. Craig, observing the daunting task ahead, gently asked, "Are you sure you want to continue?" **Determined** to reap[1] the reward for all my effort, I replied, "Absolutely, we have to go on." Step for step, Craig stayed directly behind me, providing a welcome sense of security. When I finally reached the top, I was overcome with joy. Ten months after my transplant, I had reached the top of Half Dome! My new heart had not failed me.

7   Craig and I made our way over to the edge. Pausing to peer into the valley below, we stood in silence, amazed at how far we had come. As if the moment itself was not enough, Craig surprised me with a gold charm[2] in the shape of Half Dome. He said, "This is the first mountain to add to the bracelet I gave you. . . ." As I held the handcrafted ornament in my hand, I was amazed at its likeness. It was smooth on the back, resembling the perfectly bell-shaped dome, the front being chiseled, replicating its famous broken granite face. Craig took a moment to express how proud he was of me, saying, "When you were really sick and I had to help you up the stairs at night, I always looked at the famous Ansel Adams photo of Half Dome hung on the stairway wall and wondered if we'd ever make another climb." We had done it; we were here at the top of the mountain—a long way from those nights of not knowing what the future would bring.

[1] **reap:** to receive a benefit due to one's efforts
[2] **charm:** a small piece of jewelry often worn on bracelets

Vocabulary Skill Review

In Unit 3, you learned that synonyms are words that have similar meanings. Can you think of any synonyms for the vocabulary words in Activity B?

B. VOCABULARY Complete each sentence with the vocabulary from Reading 2.

1. My _____ for this year is to train until I am ready to run the city marathon.

2. My husband took a class that helped him _____ his fear of flying. Now he can ride in airplanes without feeling so nervous.

3. We were very tired, but we didn't give up. We were _____ to get to the top of the mountain.

4. The firefighters _____ entered the burning school to rescue the children.

5. When our parents were away, my oldest brother took on the _____ of the family guardian.

6. I always recognize Dina on the phone because she has a very _____ voice. She doesn't sound like any of my other friends.

7. When we were children, we had to do work around the house in order to _____ rewards like toys or candy.

8. Rock climbing is the _____ activity for people who want a fun, exciting challenge.

9. Volunteering in South America was one of the most _____ experiences of my life. It inspired me to pursue a career in public service.

iQ ONLINE **C. Go online for more practice with the vocabulary.**

D. Read the sentences. Then number them in the order that the events happened.

____ a. Kelly decided to climb Half Dome Mountain in Yosemite.

____ b. Ten months after her heart replacement, Kelly began to climb Half Dome.

____ c. Kelly decided that she wanted to climb a mountain to change her image.

____ d. Kelly became very sick and received a heart transplant.

____ e. Craig was proud of Kelly's accomplishment.

____ f. Kelly reached the top of Half Dome with a new heart.

E. **Read the summary statements. Then write the number of the paragraph that each statement summarizes in Reading 2.**

1. I'd prefer to be challenged by mountain climbing and not illness. __2__

2. I hoped to stand tall, but imperfect, like the mountain I chose to climb. ____

3. The last part of the mountain is so steep that there are stairs to help people climb to the top, and I was going to be one of those people. ____

4. I missed extreme physical activity and needed to prove to my family and friends, and more importantly, to myself, that I could still do it. ____

F. **Complete each statement with information from Reading 2. Then write the paragraph number where the answer is found.**

1. Kelly chose a mountain to climb that is _____ feet high. ____

2. One reason she chose this mountain is because, like her, it is

   _____. ____

3. Kelly began her climb of Half Dome with her husband in August of

   _____. ____

4. The last half-mile of the climb is hard if you're afraid of heights because it's

   angled at _____ degrees. ____

5. There is a rough stairway to help climbers for the last _____ feet. ____

6. Kelly's husband Craig said it was the first mountain to add to

   _____ that he gave her. ____

G. **Read the statements. Write *T* (true) or *F* (false), and write the paragraph number where the answer is found. Then correct each false statement to make it true.**

1. Kelly didn't want her husband to climb directly behind her. _____

2. Craig was confident before this climb that they would be climbing mountains again. _____

3. Kelly had trouble when she began the climb up Half Dome Mountain.

   _____

4. Kelly used to be very athletic before she got sick. _____

5. The gloves on the stairs of Half Dome are to help people going up the mountain. _____

WRITE WHAT YOU THINK

A. Discuss the questions in a group. Look back at your Quick Write on page 115 as you think about what you learned.

1. In paragraph 2, Kelly talks about challenges—climbing mountains and being sick—and says, "Of the two, of course, I'd rather the mountain be my physical challenge than physical challenges be my 'mountain.'" What does this mean for Kelly?

2. Kelly Perkins climbed mountains before and after her heart transplant. Do you think the reasons for climbing mountains were different before and after her transplant? Why or why not?

B. Think about the unit video, Reading 1, and Reading 2 as you discuss the questions. Then choose one question and write a paragraph in response.

1. Do you think that people who do extreme sports would not be happy if they didn't continue to take risks? In other words, do you think they need to take risks?

2. Do you think people can change the way they perceive risk? Are there certain situations or times in people's lives when we perceive activities as being more or less risky?

Vocabulary Skill	Using the dictionary to find the correct meaning

Words often have more than one meaning. When dictionaries include more than one meaning, the different definitions are usually numbered. When you are using a dictionary to find the correct meaning for a word, it is important to read the entire sentence and consider the context.

Look at the example and the dictionary definitions that follow it. Definition 4 is correct.

> **Example:** Mountains began to **consume** my thoughts.

> **con·sume** AWL /kənˈsum/ *verb* [T] (*written*) **1** to use something such as fuel, energy, or time: *25 percent of the world's population consumes 80 percent of the planet's resources.* **2** to eat or drink something: *to consume calories* **3** (used about fire) to destroy something **4** (used about an emotion) to affect someone very strongly: *She was consumed by grief when her son was killed.*

All dictionary entries are from the *Oxford American Dictionary for learners of English* © Oxford University Press 2011.

A. Read these sentences from the readings. Look up the underlined words in your dictionary and write the correct definition based on the context. Then compare your answers with a partner.

1. What is it that <u>drives</u> some people to <u>embrace</u> extreme risks, while the rest of us run to the safety of the sidelines?

   drive: _____

   embrace: _____

2. He notes that most of us reach a point that limits our <u>appetite</u> for extreme risk and, as a result, our ability to perform well in dangerous conditions.

   appetite: _____

3. The fear that drives many people away from the risks of extreme sports may be the same <u>ingredient</u> that keeps others coming back for more.

   ingredient: _____

4. I had been cast in the <u>role</u> of patient.

   role: _____

5. I wanted bruises to be <u>earned</u> from sports-related activities, not from needle pricks and aspirin-thinned blood.

   earned: _____

6. It was smooth on the back, resembling the perfectly bell-shaped dome, the front being chiseled, replicating its famous broken granite <u>face</u>.

   face: _____

B. Choose three words from Activity A. Write a sentence using each word.

1. _____

   _____

2. _____

   _____

3. _____

   _____

iQ ONLINE **C.** Go online for more practice with using the dictionary to find the correct meaning.

WRITING

UNIT OBJECTIVE ▶▶▶▶ At the end of this unit, you will write a narrative essay about a risk that you have taken. This essay will include specific information from the readings and your own ideas.

Writing Skill | Writing a narrative essay

A **narrative essay** describes a personal experience. The introductory paragraph of a narrative essay gives necessary background information and then explains why this is an important or memorable story for the writer. This main idea is included in the thesis statement.

A narrative essay also contains the other important parts of an essay, including two to three body paragraphs and a concluding paragraph. The body paragraphs describe the events and include details, such as facts, examples, or explanations, to support the thesis statement or main idea of the essay. The concluding paragraph restates the main idea and summarizes why this story is an important one for the writer.

A. **WRITING MODEL** Read the model narrative essay.

When I graduated from college, I got a job working as a manager of a large restaurant. The hours were good and the pay was not bad, especially for a first job out of college. I learned a lot while working at the restaurant, but I still knew that I could do things better, or at least I thought I could. My dream had always been to open my own restaurant. An opportunity to fulfill this dream came to me one day, and I decided to take the risk and go for it.

A few years after I had been working at the restaurant, I noticed an ad in the newspaper for a restaurant that was for sale. It was a lot of money, much more than I had saved. I knew that the location of the restaurant was a good one; the restaurant had been fairly successful at that location. It could be a good investment in my future, but it was a risky, expensive one. I spoke with someone at my bank about getting a loan to purchase the restaurant, but I didn't have enough work experience or money for the bank to take a chance on my loan. I was about to give up on my dream when my father came to me and told me that he had saved some money for his retirement that I could have. He said if the restaurant was successful, I could pay him back little by little. It was a risk, but one that I was willing to take.

I was aware that statistics show that one out of three new businesses fail, but I took my father's money and bought the restaurant. With the help of my relatives, I completely changed the look of the restaurant, and three months later, it opened. It was a lot of hard work. I worked seven days a week, 10 to 12 hours a day. There were some days when I thought that maybe I should have stayed at my manager's job. There is a lot more responsibility in owning your own restaurant, and I was worried about losing my father's retirement money. What if the restaurant failed and I lost everything?

The hard work eventually paid off, and after a year, the restaurant started becoming very popular. I was even able to pay my father back. Taking a huge financial risk was scary, but fulfilling a lifelong dream gives you a feeling that can't be described. I felt that I was the luckiest person in the world.

B. **Reread the narrative essay in Activity A. Then answer the questions.**

1. Where does the writer give background information? Put a check mark (✓) next to it.

2. Which sentence in the introductory paragraph includes the main idea (thesis statement) of the narrative? Write it below.

   _____

   _____

3. How many body paragraphs does the writer include? Mark the body paragraph(s) with brackets. ([ ])

4. What details does the writer include that help make the narrative interesting? Underline them.

5. Which sentence in the concluding paragraph explains why this story is important to the writer? Write it below.

   _____

   _____

The storm began quickly and wildly. I was sitting in my living room watching the ocean as the waves grew in size and strength. Many people told me I was foolish to stay in my house and not seek shelter away from the beach. But this was my home. I had always stayed put during previous hurricanes, and this was no exception. _____

_____

The ferocious winds died down almost as quickly as they had started. As I inspected my house, I realized the basement contained two feet of water. Fortunately, I had removed anything valuable before the storm. Then I noticed the flood of water running down the street. The street was no more, replaced by a river running through the neighborhood. As I was surveying the area, I heard shouts from down the street. I walked out to the garage and grabbed my kayak. This would provide my transportation for the next few hours.

I paddled down the street to where the shouts were coming from. One of my neighbors—another risk-taker—had stayed in his house, but the water had poured into the second floor. He and his family, including two small children, were left with only the attic to stay in. I tied a rope to each of the children and placed them into the kayak. I paddled them to the end of the street where the water subsided and pavement was visible. We finally reached an undamaged home, and I lifted the children to safety. Then I returned to help their parents.

Though the flooding went on through the night, the damage had been done in minutes. Some people thought I had taken an unnecessary risk by staying in the house, but saving my neighbor and his family was proof enough for me that I had made the right decision.

1. Which sentence is the best thesis statement for the essay? Discuss your choice with a partner. Write the thesis statement in the introductory paragraph.

    a. Hurricanes are very exciting, so I wanted to stay and see as much as I could.

    b. I felt confident that nothing was going to happen to my house, so I made my decision to stay and watch it.

    c. I knew I was taking a risk, but I thought maybe I could help others who might be in need.

2. Underline any background information in the introductory paragraph.

3. Look at the concluding paragraph. Underline the words that restate the main idea and summarize why this story is important to the writer.

 D. Go online for more practice with writing a narrative essay.

A written essay or passage begins with a specific time frame, such as past, present, or future. Sometimes writers use one time frame for the entire passage, but often they shift or change time frames. Writers shift time frames according to what they are describing.

Writers often use the **simple past** to begin a story, or set the scene.

> simple past
>
> A few months after the Half Dome climb, I **decided** to climb Mt. Whitney in California.

Writers use the **past perfect** to describe things that happened before the events in the story. Use *had* + **past participle** to form the past perfect.

> simple past
>
> Secretly, I **wanted** to do something significant to help change the image that
>
> past perfect
>
> friends and family **had developed** of me.

Writers use the **simple present** to describe things or give certain facts or information.

> simple present   simple present
>
> Half Dome's shape **is** unforgettably distinctive because it**'s** broken.

A. Look back at the narrative essay on page 124. Draw a box around the simple past verbs and past perfect verbs. Circle the simple present verbs. Then compare your answers with a partner.

B. Read the short passages. Write *present* if the passage uses only a present time frame. Write *past* if the passage uses only a past time frame. Write *present/past* or *past/present* if the passage changes time frames.

1. ___past / present___ Three years ago, I went hiking in the White Mountains in New Hampshire. New Hampshire is a beautiful place to hike with lots of lakes and mountains.

2. _____ The storm last week caused a lot of damage, and many people could not get to work or school. Now the roads are clear, and businesses and schools are open again.

3. _____ Florence, Italy is a wonderful place to spend a vacation. There are lots of interesting things to do and see, and the food is delicious.

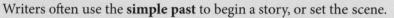

4. _____ Last year, Amy decided to try rock climbing. It was something she had never done, but had always wanted to try.

5. _____ Mountain climbing is exciting, but it can be very dangerous. Last year, there were hundreds of mountain-climbing accidents. Many of the climbers were very experienced.

C. Complete each sentence using a different time frame.

1. I used to drive to work, but now _____ I ride my bike _____.

2. I used to drink soda every day. Then my doctor told me it was bad for my health. Now _____.

3. When I was younger, I didn't speak English very well.

   Now _____.

4. Many things are different in my country now. For example, in the

   past, _____.

5. I used to eat every meal in a restaurant. I'm trying to save money,

   so now _____.

6. I used to watch TV all weekend, but now _____

   _____.

D. Go online for more practice with shifts between past and present time frames.

E. Go online for the grammar expansion.

 In this assignment, you are going to write a narrative essay about a risk you have taken. As you prepare your essay, think about the Unit Question, "Why do people take risks?" Be sure to include an introductory paragraph with the main idea of your essay, two body paragraphs, and a concluding paragraph. Use information from Reading 1, Reading 2, the unit video, and your work in this unit to support your essay. Refer to the Self-Assessment checklist on page 128.

iQ ONLINE Go to the Online Writing Tutor for a writing model and alternate Unit Assignments.

PLAN AND WRITE

A. **BRAINSTORM** Think of some risks that you've taken. They can be small or big risks. Write as many as you can.

_____

_____

_____

B. **PLAN** Follow these steps to plan your essay.

1. Look at the risks you wrote down in Activity A. Choose one of the risks to write about for your essay.

2. Write your thesis statement.

_____

_____

iQ ONLINE 3. Go to the Online Resources to download and complete the outline for your narrative essay.

iQ ONLINE **C.** **WRITE** Use your **PLAN** notes to write your essay. Go to *iQ Online* to use the Online Writing Tutor.

1. Write your narrative essay describing a risk you have taken.

2. Look at the Self-Assessment checklist on page 128 to guide your writing.

REVISE AND EDIT

A. PEER REVIEW Read your partner's essay. Then go online and use the Peer Review worksheet. Discuss the review with your partner.

B. REWRITE Based on your partner's review, revise and rewrite your essay.

C. EDIT Complete the Self-Assessment checklist as you prepare to write the final draft of your essay. Be prepared to hand in your work or discuss it in class.

SELF-ASSESSMENT		
Yes	No	
☐	☐	Does the essay begin with an introductory paragraph that gives the reason you took the risk and any important background information?
☐	☐	Does the essay include two body paragraphs that describe the events and provide details?
☐	☐	Does the essay contain a concluding paragraph that restates why you took the risk and summarizes why the story is important to you?
☐	☐	Does the essay shift between present and past correctly?
☐	☐	Are words used with the correct meaning?
☐	☐	Does the essay include vocabulary from the unit?
☐	☐	Did you check the essay for punctuation, spelling, and grammar?

D. REFLECT Go to the Online Discussion Board to discuss these questions.

1. What is something new you learned in this unit?

2. Look back at the Unit Question—Why do people take risks? Is your answer different now than when you started the unit? If yes, how is it different? Why?

TRACK YOUR SUCCESS

Circle the words you have learned in this unit.

Nouns
appetite
aspect 🔑 AWL
challenge 🔑 AWL
face 🔑
goal 🔑 AWL
ingredient 🔑
precaution
pursuit AWL
role 🔑 AWL

tolerance
trait

Verbs
conquer
consume AWL
drive 🔑
earn 🔑
embrace
perceive AWL

Adjectives
determined 🔑
distinctive AWL
mental 🔑 AWL
notable
significant 🔑 AWL
ultimate 🔑 AWL
vivid

Adverb
bravely

🔑 Oxford 3000™ words
AWL Academic Word List

Check (✓) the skills you learned. If you need more work on a skill, refer to the page(s) in parentheses.

READING	■	I can use referents to understand contrast. (p. 113)
VOCABULARY	■	I can use the dictionary to find correct meanings. (p. 120)
WRITING	■	I can write a narrative essay. (p. 122)
GRAMMAR	■	I can use time shifts correctly in narrative writing. (p. 125)
UNIT OBJECTIVE ▶▶▶▶	■	I can gather information and ideas to write a narrative essay about a risk I have taken.

READING ▶ using a graphic organizer
VOCABULARY ▶ phrasal verbs
WRITING ▶ stating reasons and giving examples
GRAMMAR ▶ gerunds and infinitives

UNIT QUESTION

Why do people help each other?

A Discuss these questions with your classmates.

1. Did your parents teach you to be helpful to others? Is being helpful something we learn, or is it human nature?

2. Are there any situations in which you don't think you should help someone? Explain.

3. Look at the photo. What do you think is happening?

B Listen to *The Q Classroom* online. Then answer these questions.

1. Sophy and Yuna suggest that it is in people's nature to help other people. In what situations do you think people naturally want to help others?

2. Felix states that we help others to feel good about ourselves. What point could you add to the discussion to show you agree or disagree?

 C Go to the Online Discussion Board to discuss the Unit Question with your classmates.

D Discuss these questions with a partner.

1. What are some situations in which you need help?

2. What are some situations in which other people need help?

3. Read the list of situations. Would you help? Why or why not?
   - A homeless person is asking for money.
   - A tourist is looking at a map on a street corner.
   - A child falls down.

E Look at the pictures below. Discuss these questions in a group.

1. What is happening in each picture? Where are these situations taking place?

2. Why do people help strangers in these situations?

3. Have you helped others in a similar way? Explain.

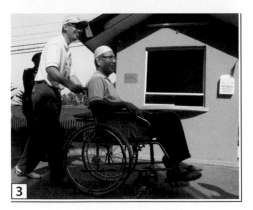

READING 1 | A Question of Numbers

You are going to read an article from a news magazine that presents research on the *bystander effect*. The bystander effect describes how a group of ordinary people, suddenly in an emergency situation, reacts when help is needed. Use the article to gather information and ideas for your Unit Assignment.

PREVIEW THE READING

A. **PREVIEW** Read the title and look at the photograph. When do you think a person is more likely to help other people? Check (✓) your answer.

☐ when he or she is alone

☐ when there are many people around

B. **QUICK WRITE** When do you ask for help from family and friends? When do you ask for help from strangers? Write for 5–10 minutes in response. Be sure to use this section for your Unit Assignment.

C. **VOCABULARY** Check (✓) the words you know. Then work with a partner to locate each word in the reading. Use clues to help define the words you don't know. Check your definitions in the dictionary.

according to (phr.) 🔑	end up (phr. v.) 🔑	responsibility (n.) 🔑
apply to (phr. v.) 🔑	factor (n.) 🔑	theory (n.) 🔑
complex (adj.) 🔑	prove (v.) 🔑	witness (n.) 🔑

🔑 Oxford 3000™ words

ONLINE **D.** Go online to listen and practice your pronunciation.

WORK WITH THE READING

◎ **A.** Read the article and gather information about why people help each other.

A Question of Numbers

1   You're walking down a busy city sidewalk, and you see someone in front of you fall down. What would you do? Now imagine that same situation, but you are the only other person on the sidewalk. What would you do then? **According to** social psychologists, you are more likely to help when there is no one else around. In contrast, if there are many **witnesses**, or bystanders, you might not offer help. It is even possible that no one would help the person at all. Psychologists believe this is a natural yet **complex** human reaction, which they call the *bystander effect*.

2   The bystander effect was first discovered in 1964 as a result of a very unfortunate event that happened outside Catherine Genovese's home in New York City. At three o'clock in the morning, someone attacked and murdered Genovese in front of her apartment building. The noise of the killing woke up 38 of Genovese's neighbors. All of them looked out of their windows to see what was happening. However, not one of those 38 witnesses did anything to help. No one reported the murder to the police. The whole nation was shocked by the news the next day, and psychologists had no answers to explain why these people didn't help.

3   Newspapers called the 38 witnesses selfish and uncaring, but social psychologists John Darley and Bibb Latane had a different **theory**. They believed that a large number of witnesses actually *decreased* the chances that any individual would help. If only one person witnesses a murder, he or she will feel fully responsible for calling the police. If there are two witnesses, each person might feel only half responsible. Now imagine there are many witnesses, as in the Genovese case. Darley and Latane pointed out that each person felt only a small amount of **responsibility**, so each did nothing. The reason they didn't help was not that they were uncaring or selfish people. There were just too many of them.

4   Darley and Latane knew they had to **prove** their theory scientifically, so they set up an experiment with college students to test it. They divided the students into three groups. They took each student to a small building. They put him or her in a room with a TV screen that showed another person in a different room in the building; then they left. Students in the first group thought that they were alone in the building. Students in the second group thought that there was one other person in the building. Students in the third group thought that there were four other people in the building. As part of the experiment, the person on the TV screen pretended[1] to become ill and called out for help. In the first group, where students

---

[1] **pretend:** to behave as if something is true or real, when it is not

believed they were the only people in the building, 85 percent went to get help for the person. In the second group, only 62 percent tried to help. In the third group, only 31 percent tried to help. The results supported Darley and Latane's theory. They figured out that having more witnesses did not mean that help was more likely. In fact, the opposite was true.

5   Social psychologists believe the bystander effect can **apply to** a number of everyday situations. For example, on a busy sidewalk, you might not give money to a homeless man (or help someone who falls down). On a crowded subway, you may not give up your seat to an elderly person. On the highway, you might choose not to stop and help someone change a flat tire. In these situations, you—and the other bystanders—feel less responsible because so many people are around to help, so no one **ends up** helping at all.

6   The bystander effect is one of the many **factors** that influence a person's decision to help out a stranger in need. Some people might naturally feel more desire to help. Some cultures might put more importance on helping strangers than others do. Some cities and towns could

The bystander effect is common on busy city streets.

be designed to be more friendly than others. However, psychologists know that humans are naturally influenced by the presence of others around them even if they are not aware of it.

Vocabulary Skill Review

In Unit 4, you learned how to identify noun and adjective suffixes. Which words in the sentences in Activity B have a noun suffix? Which have an adjective suffix?

B. VOCABULARY Complete each sentence with the vocabulary from Reading 1. You may need to change the form of the word or phrase to make the sentence grammatically correct.

according to (*phr.*)	end up (*phr. v.*)	responsibility (*n.*)
apply to (*phr. v.*)	factor (*n.*)	theory (*n.*)
complex (*adj.*)	prove (*v.*)	witness (*n.*)

1. _____ social psychologists, cultures have different ideas about what behaviors are considered acceptable and unacceptable.

2. The police knew it would be useful to talk to the _____ who saw the thief steal the woman's purse.

3. Human relationships are _____. They are not easy to explain.

4. Scientists use a(n) _____ to explain why something happens. Then they test the idea to see whether or not it is true.

5. In some cultures, people greatly value kindness to others and feel it is their _____ to help their neighbors as much as they can.

6. Scientists must do experiments in order to _____ that their ideas are correct.

7. Successful experiments usually have expected results, but scientists can sometimes _____ discovering something completely new or unexpected from an experiment.

8. Scientists who study people's behavior look at many different _____ that can affect behavior, such as gender and culture.

9. Some biologists study the way our biology affects our behavior; in contrast, social psychologists examine the way our actions _____ society.

iQ ONLINE **C.** **Go online for more practice with the vocabulary.**

D. **Read the statements. Write _T_ (true) or _F_ (false). Then correct each false statement to make it true according to the article.**

_____ 1. The bystander effect is a natural human reaction that occurs in situations in which help is needed.

_____ 2. None of the witnesses to Catherine Genovese's murder called the police.

_____ 3. Social psychologists studied the bystander effect before the murder of Catherine Genovese.

_____ 4. Darley and Latane's experiment showed that having more witnesses meant that help was less likely.

_____ 5. The number of people who witness an emergency will affect the amount of responsibility each witness feels.

_____ 6. Darley and Latane studied the bystander effect by watching how people behave in everyday situations.

_____ 7. The bystander effect is one of the factors that influence people's decision to help others.

_____ 8. People almost always help a stranger when there are other people around.

E. Read the statements. Then check (✓) the implied main idea of the paragraph.

1. Paragraph 2

   ☐ a. Catherine Genovese was murdered outside her apartment building at three o'clock in the morning.

   ☐ b. The witnesses to Catherine Genovese's murder looked out their windows to see what was happening.

   ☐ c. People could not explain why the witnesses to Catherine Genovese's murder did nothing to help her.

   ☐ d. When Catherine Genovese was murdered, 38 of her neighbors woke up from the noise.

2. Paragraph 3

   ☐ a. Darley and Latane's theory suggests that a bystander feels responsible when there are no other witnesses, but not responsible when there is one other witness.

   ☐ b. According to Darley and Latane's theory, people feel little responsibility when there are many witnesses, which explains why the 38 witnesses to Catherine Genovese's murder did nothing.

   ☐ c. Social psychologists like John Darley and Bibb Latane develop theories to explain how people act in various situations and why they react to situations in different ways.

   ☐ d. Many people agreed with the newspapers that the 38 witnesses in Catherine Genovese's apartment building were selfish, but Darley and Latane did not share their opinion.

3. Paragraph 4

   ☐ a. Darley and Latane put college students in different rooms to test their theory of the bystander effect.

   ☐ b. Students in Darley and Latane's experiment were divided into three groups.

   ☐ c. Students in the first group helped more often than those in the second and third groups.

   ☐ d. Darley and Latane's experiment with college students proved their theory of the bystander effect.

F. Circle the answer that best completes each statement.

1. Catherine Genovese's murder occurred ____.
   a. outside New York City
   b. in her apartment
   c. in front of her apartment building
   d. on the street

2. When only one person witnesses a crime, he or she will feel ____ for calling the police.
   a. not at all responsible
   b. partly responsible
   c. less responsible
   d. more responsible

3. Darley and Latane's experiment divided college students into ____ groups.
   a. two
   b. three
   c. four
   d. five

4. Students in the third group believed that ____ other people were in the building.
   a. no
   b. two
   c. three
   d. four

5. In Darley and Latane's experiment, ____ of the students who thought they were alone went to get help for the person pretending to be ill.
   a. 85 percent
   b. 62 percent
   c. 38 percent
   d. 31 percent

G. Read the sentences from Reading 1. Choose the statement that you can infer from each sentence.

1. (Paragraph 1) Psychologists believe this is a natural yet complex human reaction, which they call the bystander effect.
   a. The bystander effect occurs in bad situations.
   b. The bystander effect doesn't happen often.
   c. The bystander effect is difficult to understand.

2. (Paragraph 2) The whole nation was shocked by the news the next day, and psychologists had no answers to explain why these people didn't help.
   a. Only people in New York heard about the murder.
   b. News about the murder traveled quickly.
   c. The murder was not shocking to psychologists.

3. (Paragraph 4) Darley and Latane knew they had to prove their theory scientifically, so they set up an experiment with college students to test it.
   a. Darley and Latane paid the college students to participate.
   b. Darley and Latane's theory had already been proven.
   c. People would not believe Darley and Latane without proof.

4. (Paragraph 4) In the third group, only 31 percent tried to help.
   a. More people decided not to help.
   b. The third group had many people.
   c. Thirty-one percent was a big number.

5. (Paragraph 5) Social psychologists believe the bystander effect can apply to a number of everyday situations.
   a. The number of everyday situations is low.
   b. The number of everyday situations varies.
   c. The number of everyday situations is high.

6. (Paragraph 6) The bystander effect is one of the many factors that influence a person's decision to help out a stranger in need.
   a. The bystander effect influences people's decisions to help strangers more than other factors.
   b. The bystander effect is not the only factor influencing people's decisions to help strangers.
   c. The bystander effect has the most influence on people's decisions to help strangers.

H. Do you think the bystander effect is a good excuse for not helping a stranger in need? Write 5–8 sentences giving your opinion.

I. Go online to read *Voluntary Service Overseas* and check your comprehension.

WRITE WHAT YOU THINK

A. Discuss these questions in a group.

1. Have you ever *not* helped someone who needed help? Why or why not? What factors might make someone choose not to help a stranger?

2. In general, which people do you think are more helpful to strangers in need: people who live in cities or people who live in small towns? Why?

3. The author of "A Question of Numbers" writes that "some cultures might put more importance on helping strangers than others do." Do you think that a person's culture can be a factor in making him or her a more helpful person? Why or why not?

B. Choose one question and write a paragraph in response. Look back at your Quick Write on page 133 as you think about what you learned.

Graphic organizers represent ideas with images, such as diagrams, charts, tables, and timelines. You can use graphic organizers to help you see connections between ideas or remember the main points of a text or parts of a text. Using graphic organizers can help you review a text you have read in preparation for class or a test.

This flowchart organizes the main points of a scientific article.

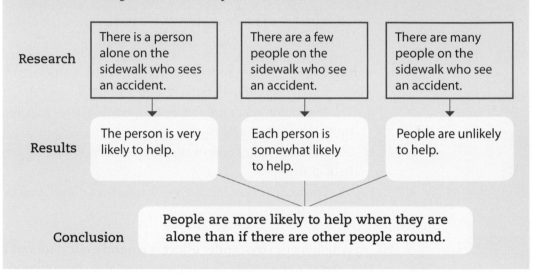

Critical Thinking (Tip)

Activity A uses a graphic organizer to **illustrate** the ideas of a reading. When you illustrate, you make a picture of information or ideas. This is a good way to understand material and to review for a test.

A. With a partner, complete a student's flowchart for paragraph 4 of Reading 1. Then discuss the questions below.

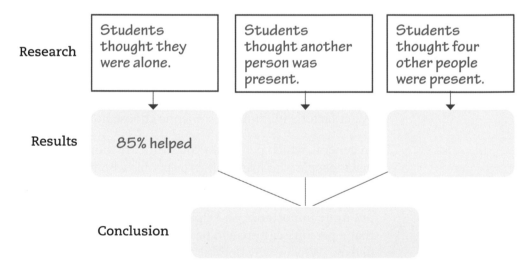

(Tip) **for Success**

Looking for patterns of organization in a text will help you understand what the writer wants to say about the topic.

1. How does the flowchart organize information from the reading?

2. Look at the labels on the left. Are these words from the reading or from the student who made the flowchart?

3. Does the flowchart make the information easier to understand?

B. Work with a partner. Use the flowchart from Activity A. Complete the summary of paragraph 4 of Reading 1.

Darley and Latane researched the bystander effect using _____

1

groups of students in different situations. When students thought they

were _____, 85 percent tried to help someone in need. When they

2

thought one other person was present, _____ tried to help. Finally,

3

only 31 percent helped when students thought _____ other people

4

were present. Based on these results, Darley and Latane concluded that

_____.

5

 **C.** Go online for more practice using a graphic organizer.

READING 2 | The Biology of Altruism

You are going to read an article from a science journal that presents research on how the brain can influence a person's decision to help strangers. Use the article to gather information and ideas for your Unit Assignment.

PREVIEW THE READING

A. PREVIEW Read the first and last paragraphs. Why do you think people want to help strangers? Check (✓) your answer(s).

☐ It makes them feel good.   ☐ They want something in return.

☐ It helps people survive.   ☐ It makes them feel important.

☐ They feel they have to.   ☐ It is polite.

B. QUICK WRITE Why do people donate to charities? Write for 5–10 minutes in response. Be sure to use this section for your Unit Assignment.

C. VOCABULARY Check (✓) the words you know. Then work with a partner to locate each word in the reading.

altruistic (adj.)	compassionate (adj.)	rely on (phr. v.) 🔑
barely (adv.) 🔑	hypothesize (v.)	subject (n.) 🔑
bring about (phr. v.)	initial (adj.) 🔑	

🔑 Oxford 3000™ words

 D. Go online to listen and practice your pronunciation.

WORK WITH THE READING

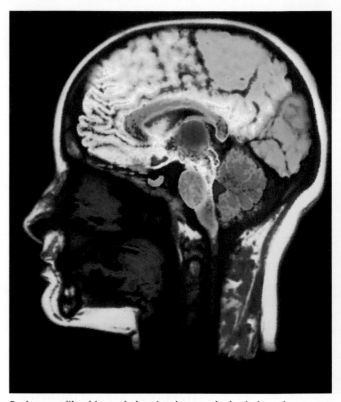

A. Read the article and gather information about why people help each other.

The Biology of Altruism

1   Scientific evidence suggests that humans have a biological desire to help others, including strangers. **Altruistic** behavior towards strangers is uniquely human and observed at a very young age. Dr. Felix Warneken and Dr. Michael Tomasello of Germany's Max Planck Institute for Evolutionary Anthropology have shown that children as young as 18 months want to help strangers. When their 18-month-old **subjects** saw a stranger throw a pencil on the floor, none of them picked it up. However, when the same subjects saw someone "accidentally" drop a pencil, nearly all the children picked it up in the first ten seconds. Says Dr. Warneken, "The results were astonishing because these children are so young. They still wear diapers and are **barely** able to use language, but they already show helping behavior." Because altruistic behavior appears in children so young, Dr. Warneken and other scientists **hypothesize** that the human brain is designed to be altruistic.

Brain scans like this one help scientists see the brain in action.

Mirror Neurons

2   By using brain scans[1], neuroscientists are making new discoveries about the biology of the human brain. The recent discovery of mirror neurons in humans leads to scientists' belief that the brain can influence altruistic behavior. Mirror neurons are ordinary brain cells located throughout the brain. They "light up" when a person is performing an action or observing someone else doing a similar action. Mirror neurons make us cry when we see someone else cry or smile when someone smiles at us. Our mirror neurons actually feel what they feel. They cry and smile along with them.

3   How, then, can mirror neurons **bring about** altruistic behavior? By helping us feel what others feel, mirror neurons naturally make us feel **compassionate**. They allow us to put ourselves in someone else's situation; without them, we would not understand or care about other people's emotions. Would we help hurricane victims[2]? Give money

---

[1] **brain scan:** an image of the brain taken by a special machine

[2] **victim:** a person harmed or killed as a result of a crime or accident

to the poor? Save lives? Probably not, says Marco Iacoboni, a leading neuroscientist: "We are good because our biology drives[3] us to be good." In other words, mirror neurons seem to prepare us to be altruistic.

Neuroeconomics

4   Neuroeconomist Bill Harbaugh and his team at the University of Oregon study the biology of altruism. They look specifically at neuroeconomics, or the connection between the brain and economic decisions. In one of their experiments, the researchers tried seeing if people's donations to charity[4] were affected by neurons. Nineteen women were given $100 to play a charity game on the computer. They could choose to donate or not to a charity, each decision leading to other situations where they could gain or lose money. At the end of the game, the subjects were able to keep all the money that was left in their accounts.

5   As the subjects played the game, the scientists scanned their brains. They looked at the brain's "pleasure center," which controls how good people feel. When most subjects donated money to a charity, their pleasure centers lit up on the brain scan. Some even lit up when the subjects were taxed on their donation. Both results suggest that the brain's pleasure center is rewarded for altruistic acts. In addition, the more people donated, the more their pleasure centers lit up. For some, the pleasure center lit up more when the computer gave the charity extra money than when they received extra money to keep for themselves. The scientists point out that this was "the first neural evidence for . . . pure altruism," meaning that altruism may indeed have a biological connection.

Unanswered Questions

6   Why would our brains be biologically prepared to help others? What benefit does it have for each of us and for human beings as a whole? One popular scientific theory suggests that being natural helpers improves our chances of survival. Humans are social creatures, dependent on family, friends, governments, and strangers. Babies need food to survive, but they also need someone there to feed them. Larger social groups also **rely on** our help, such as when we pay taxes or donate money to charities. Without a "helping brain," humans would have a much harder time trying to survive.

7   The study of the biology of altruism still has a long way to go, however. Many questions have grown out of these **initial** studies. For instance, if humans are born with a "helping" brain, why do we also have the ability to hurt others? Why are some of us more altruistic than others? How much control does the brain have on altruistic behavior? How much influence does society have? As technology advances, scientists hope to find answers to these questions and increase our understanding of ourselves.

[3] **drive:** to motivate, or cause someone to act in a particular way
[4] **charity:** an organization set up to help people in need

B. **VOCABULARY** Here are some words and phrases from Reading 2. Read the sentences. Circle the answer that best matches the meaning of each bold word or phrase. Then compare your answers with a partner.

1. The man who saved the child's life received a medal for his **altruistic** act.

   a. worried about what others will think of you   b. caring about others with no advantage for yourself   c. shy and not very sociable

2. Each **subject** in the medical study was paid $50 for answering questions about his or her health.

   a. a person who works in hospitals   b. a person who is part of an experiment   c. a person who doesn't have enough money

3. The researcher could **barely** hear anything because there was so much noise coming from outside.

   a. hardly; almost not   b. completely   c. often

4. Some scientists **hypothesize** that natural instincts and how we are raised have an equal effect on how helpful we are. Others believe one has more influence than the other.

   a. state that something is definitely true   b. suggest a possible explanation   c. disagree strongly with someone

5. Watching people on a crowded sidewalk can **bring about** a better understanding of how the bystander effect works in real life.

   a. cause   b. destroy something   c. improve the look of something

6. Healthcare workers are usually **compassionate** people—they want to help others in need.

   a. caring about other people's feelings   b. having enough money   c. taking more than your fair share

7. All scientists **rely on** experiments to test whether their ideas are true or false. They never guess that an idea is right before testing it.

   a. use occasionally   b. need and depend on   c. think about

8. The results of the **initial** study were correct because every study after it showed the same conclusions.

   a. last in a series   b. something that is at the beginning; first   c. of little importance

 C. Go online for more practice with the vocabulary.

D. Circle the answer to each question.

1. What is the main idea of the reading?
   a. Research suggests that the brain influences our desire to help others.
   b. Humans survive because they are natural helpers.
   c. Children as young as 18 months have the desire to help strangers.
   d. Brain scans are helping scientists discover more about altruistic behavior.

2. Which of the following is *not* true about mirror neurons?
   a. They light up when a person is doing something.
   b. They make us feel compassionate toward others.
   c. They make us smile when someone smiles at us.
   d. They are different from ordinary brain cells.

3. What is neuroeconomics?
   a. the study of how the brain makes decisions about money
   b. the study of how the brain controls donations to charities
   c. the study of how the brain's pleasure center works
   d. the study of how the brain makes people feel good

4. What did Dr. Harbaugh's study reveal about neuroeconomics?
   a. Some people get pleasure from being taxed on donations.
   b. The brain's pleasure center is not rewarded for altruistic acts.
   c. Donating money does not light up the brain's pleasure center.
   d. The brain's pleasure center always lights up when people donate money.

5. Why might people be born with a "helping brain"?
   a. Human babies need parents to feed them.
   b. It causes people to donate to charities.
   c. People have to live and work with others.
   d. It improves people's chances of survival.

E. Read the statements. Write *T* (true) or *F* (false). Then correct each false statement to make it true.

_____ 1. When 18-month-old subjects saw a stranger throw a pencil on the floor, they picked it up immediately.

_____ 2. Scientists believe that the brain can influence human behavior.

_____ 3. Scientists have known about mirror neurons for hundreds of years.

_____ 4. Without mirror neurons, we probably would not understand or care about other people's emotions.

_____ 5. In Harbaugh's experiment, women got $1,000 to play a charity game.

Writing **Tip**

On page 140, you learned that readers use graphic organizers to help them see connections between ideas in a text. Writers also use graphic organizers. Use a graphic organizer when you brainstorm ideas about your topic to help you organize your ideas.

F. Complete the graphic organizer for paragraph 5 of Reading 2. Look at the Reading Skill on page 140 to help you.

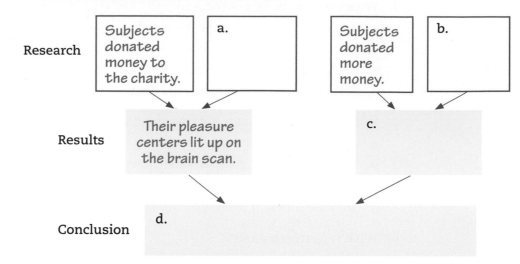

G. Work with a partner. Use the graphic organizer from Activity F. Complete the summary of paragraph 5 of Reading 2.

Neuroeconomist Bill Harbaugh researched how the brain makes economic decisions using a charity game on a computer. He found that subjects' pleasure centers lit up on a brain scan both when they donated money to a charity and when _____. Furthermore, when subjects donated more money, _____. This also happened in cases where _____ _____. Based on these results, scientists concluded that _____ _____ .

WRITE WHAT YOU THINK

A. Discuss the questions in a group. Look back at your Quick Write on page 141 as you think about what you learned.

1. How altruistic do you think you are? Give examples to support your opinion.

2. Why do you think some people are more altruistic than others?

B. Before you watch the video, discuss the questions in a group.

1. If you found a wallet on the street, what would you do with it?

2. Do you think people have a social responsibility to return lost items to their owners? Explain.

C. Go online to watch the video about altruism in Japan. Then check your comprehension.

empathy *(n.)* the ability to understand how other people feel

social contract *(n.)* an unofficial agreement shared by everyone in a society

violate *(v.)* to not respect something

D. Think about the unit video, Reading 1, and Reading 2 as you discuss the questions. Then choose one question and write a paragraph in response.

1. Which do you think has more influence on our decision to help other people: the presence of others or human nature?

2. Can a person's own life experiences make him or her a more helpful person? Explain, using examples from your own observations and experiences.

Vocabulary Skill Phrasal verbs

A **phrasal verb** is a combination of a verb and a particle. Particles are usually prepositions, such as *up*, *on*, *in*, *down*, and *over*. When they are combined with a verb, however, they can change the meaning of the verb.

Compare these pairs of sentences.

> The scientist was finished with her research, so she **ended** the experiments.
> He tried to help the old man find the address, but he **ended up** taking him home.

> Bob and Al like to **watch** ice hockey on the weekends.
> **Watch out** for that rock! It looks as if it's going to fall!

The phrasal verb *end up* has a different meaning from the verb *end*.

> end   →   to finish
> end up   →   to be in a situation after a series of events

The phrasal verb *watch out* has a different meaning from the verb *watch*.

> watch   →   to look carefully or with interest at something
> watch out   →   to be careful about something

A. Match each phrasal verb with its definition below. Look back at the readings or use your dictionary to help you.

____ 1. set up (Reading 1, para. 4) ____ 4. help out (Reading 1, para. 6)

____ 2. call out (Reading 1, para. 4) ____ 5. point out (Reading 2, para. 5)

____ 3. figure out (Reading 1, para. 4) ____ 6. grow out of (Reading 2, para. 7)

a. to tell or show something that people didn't know or think about

b. to develop from

c. to find an answer to something or to understand

d. to prepare something

e. to assist somebody

f. to say something loudly or shout in order to attract attention

B. Complete this short article wth phrasal verbs from Activity A.

Darley and Latane _____ experiments with college

1

students to _____ why no bystanders reacted to the murder

2

of Catherine Genovese. Their study helped _____ new

3

information that they didn't expect. They discovered that the presence

of more people at a scene makes people feel less responsible. The study

also showed that people in groups don't react to a problem if nobody

else acts or looks concerned. They assume that nothing is wrong, even if

they hear someone _____ for help. There have been other

4

experiments since Darley and Latane's findings. Probably even more

studies will _____ their research because psychologists are

5

very interested in knowing more about what other factors affect people's

decisions to _____ those in need.

6

iQ ONLINE **C.** Go online for more practice with phrasal verbs.

WRITING

UNIT OBJECTIVE ▶▶▶▶ At the end of this unit, you will write an analysis essay using reasons and examples about why people help each other. This essay will include specific information from the readings and your own ideas.

Writing Skill | **Stating reasons and giving examples**

An **analysis essay** is a piece of writing that carefully examines a topic by breaking it down into smaller parts. The writer looks at the smaller parts in separate body paragraphs and explains them so the reader will understand the main topic. To help explain the topic and pieces, the writer states reasons and gives examples.

Writers state **reasons** to explain why something happens. Reasons can explain why people act or do things in a certain way or why things happen. Writers support their reasons with **examples**. Examples can be specific situations or personal observations that writers give to make their reasons clearer.

> **Thesis statement** (situation): Some people don't know their neighbors very well.
>
> **Topic sentence** (Reason 1): One reason is that they might not see each other often.
> **Example:** They work so much that they are rarely at home during the day.
> **Example:** They prefer not to spend much time outside.
>
> **Topic sentence** (Reason 2): Another reason is they make the wrong assumptions about their neighbors.
> **Example:** They think their neighbors are unfriendly when in fact they are really just shy.
> **Example:** They assume their neighbors are not interested in being friends.

There are certain phrases that signal examples, such as:

> For example,   For instance,

Stating reasons with _because_

Because is often used to show reasons why something happens or is true.
When *because* is at the beginning of a sentence, a comma is put before the second subject-verb combination.

>   reason   second subject-verb combination
> <u>Because they don't feel safe themselves,</u> they don't think they can help someone else.

When *because* is in the middle of a sentence, no comma is used.

>   reason
> People may not help because they don't feel safe.

A. WRITING MODEL **Read the model analysis essay. Underline the thesis statement.**

When We Don't Help

1   We see people who need help all the time. Many times it is a friend or family member, but other times it is a complete stranger. Maybe a tourist is lost and needs directions, or maybe someone's car stopped working. Or worse yet, maybe we see a car accident and the driver is injured. In all those moments, we have to ask ourselves whether or not to help that person we don't know. Often the decision is made in a matter of seconds, and we have little time to think things through. On many occasions, people might decide not to help a stranger in need for a number of reasons.

2   One reason is that we might be too busy to help. For example, people might not stop to help a stranded driver on the side of the road because they are in a hurry to get to work. Frequently, college students are very busy and might not be able to help. For instance, students with only ten minutes to get to their next class might ignore a new student who is clearly walking around lost and confused. In these situations, ten minutes just isn't enough time to both get to class and help that lost student.

3   Second of all, people may not help in certain situations because they don't feel safe. For instance, when people hear a neighbor scream in the middle of the night, they might feel too scared to help out. They may worry about getting hurt. Since they don't feel safe themselves, they don't think they can help someone else. Another example is when people see a fight on the street or sidewalk. Trying to stop the fight could be unsafe. If bystanders get involved, they could get injured. Instead, they decide not to help in order to stay safe.

4   Finally, we might not help others because we assume they can help themselves. For example, if someone on the sidewalk seems to be lost, people may think that he or she can find the necessary information without their help. This is especially true today since many people have smartphones with instant access to online maps. Age is another factor. For instance, people would probably help an old man who accidently falls down on the sidewalk, but if a young man falls, they might do nothing. This happens because they think he can get up by himself.

5   Overall, the decision not to help is very complex. Time, safety, and thinking people can help themselves are just three of many reasons a person chooses not to help others. When it comes to helping strangers, we have to consider many different factors, and we usually have very little time to try to make the right decision. However, that is what makes human psychology so fascinating. Many times there is no right answer, and in the end, we just have to listen to our inner voice and do what we think is best.

B. Complete the graphic organizer with information from the essay in Activity A.

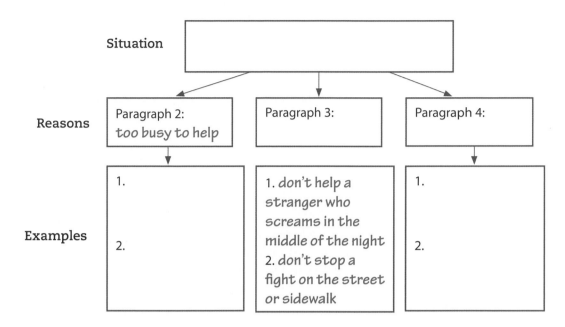

Situation

Reasons

Paragraph 2:
too busy to help

Paragraph 3:

Paragraph 4:

Examples

1.

2.

1. *don't help a stranger who screams in the middle of the night*
2. *don't stop a fight on the street or sidewalk*

1.

2.

C. WRITING MODEL Read the model analysis essay. On page 152, choose the best example for the reason in each body paragraph.

Why People Volunteer Overseas

1   It is estimated that over one million people volunteer overseas each year. Many of these volunteers travel thousands of miles to other countries all across Africa, Asia, and Latin America. They experience foreign cultures and visit beautiful places. However, volunteering in a foreign country is not just for the fun of international travel. In fact, people volunteer overseas for several important reasons.

2   One of the main reasons people volunteer overseas is to give back to those in need. For example, many volunteers travel to poorer countries where people don't have basic conveniences that are found in other countries. Some build wells to give small villages access to clean water. Others set up medical clinics so people can get treatment for common illnesses like the flu. Many of these volunteers come from countries with good schools, and they want to give others the same educational opportunities. Overall, these volunteers feel they have a responsibility to people who deserve the same opportunities they have back home.

3   Second of all, many volunteers feel that traveling overseas can improve their job skills. These volunteers can add their international experiences to their résumés. This is important because many companies today are looking for employees who have a global perspective. Volunteering

overseas also teaches people how to work effectively on a team, which helps when applying for future jobs. Learning about teamwork in a foreign setting will make these volunteers stand out from the crowd when they apply for jobs.

4   A third reason people volunteer in foreign countries is because they want to immerse themselves in a foreign culture. Living in another country is one of the most rewarding experiences a person can have. Being a part of a new culture for even a short period of time will bring these volunteers a sense of belonging and a deeper level of understanding of how people live in other parts of the world.

5   In addition to experiencing the new country, volunteers also get time away from their modern, fast-paced lifestyles back home. The majority of volunteers come from Canada, the United Kingdom, and the United States, where people are often rushing around and feeling stressed. When these volunteers spend time in a country with a slower pace of life, they feel less stress and can enjoy a different lifestyle. This shows that volunteering abroad can be good for both the mind and the body.

6   Overseas volunteers do not just travel for fun. They travel with a purpose. All these volunteers travel because they want to help others in some way. At the same time, they are gaining valuable work and life experiences. It's hard to ask for anything more than that.

____ Paragraph 2   a. For example, a volunteer teacher will need to work together with local teachers and administrators. As a result, he or she will gain valuable experience in making decisions as a group.

____ Paragraph 3   b. For instance, having time to talk with people, ride a bicycle, or take long walks could help an office worker with a busy, stressful job to feel better and more relaxed.

____ Paragraph 4   c. For example, volunteers may try different foods and ways of having fun. They will work and form friendships with people who think and do things differently.

____ Paragraph 5   d. For instance, they often teach mathematics or English in local schools that lack qualified teachers. Some help build new schools for children.

D. Read the sentences. Underline the reasons. Add commas if needed.

1. <u>Because the witnesses didn't feel responsible</u>, they did nothing to help.

2. Because our brains have mirror neurons we can feel what others feel.

3. The scientists performed an experiment because they wanted to prove their theory.

4. Altruistic behavior is complex because many factors are involved.

5. People might help others because it improves their chances of survival.

6. Because the street was so busy no one noticed the man.

 E. Go online for more practice with stating reasons and giving examples.

Grammar | Gerunds and infinitives

A **gerund** is the base form of a **verb + -ing**. Gerunds function as nouns in a sentence. A gerund can be one word (*running, eating, living*) or part of a phrase (*running outdoors, eating healthily, living in a big city*).

Gerunds as subjects

A gerund or **gerund phrase** can be the subject of a sentence. A gerund subject always takes a singular verb.

Helping <u>is</u> easier when we feel safe.
Being altruistic <u>means</u> helping others without expecting anything in return.

Gerunds after verbs

Gerunds follow certain verbs. Here are some of the verbs that gerunds follow:

avoid	discuss	enjoy	go	quit
consider	dislike	finish	practice	suggest

An **infinitive** is *to* + **the base form** of a verb. Infinitives can also function as nouns in sentences.

They wanted **to donate** money.

Infinitives after verbs

Infinitives follow certain verbs. Here are some of the verbs that infinitives follow:

agree	decide	hope	plan	wait
appear	forget	learn	seem	want

A. Complete each sentence with a gerund phrase. Use the words in parentheses.

1. _Understanding human behavior_ (understand/human behavior) is not always easy.

2. _____ (help/other people) is part of human nature.

3. _____ (donate/money) is an example of altruistic behavior.

4. _____ (use/brain scans) has helped scientists better understand human behavior.

5. _____ (live/in a big city) can be stressful.

B. Complete each sentence with a verb + a gerund.

1. I wanted to be healthier, but I really _dislike exercising_ (dislike/exercise).

2. If you have heart problems, you should _____ (quit/eat) salty foods.

3. Ahmed _____ (consider/move) to Riyadh, but he decided to stay in Jeddah.

4. We should _____ (avoid/buy) a big car. Gasoline is too expensive.

5. Today we will _____ (discuss/write) paragraphs.

6. After Margo _____ (finish/eat) dinner, she read the newspaper.

C. Complete each sentence with a gerund or an infinitive.

1. I hope _____to go_____ (go) to Australia someday.

2. Yuri wants _____ (visit) his friend in Seoul next fall.

3. You should practice _____ (speak) Spanish every day.

4. My neighbor agreed _____ (help) me fix my car.

5. Do you enjoy _____ (play) soccer?

6. Jamal goes _____ (swim) every morning with his son.

iQ ONLINE **D.** Go online for more practice with gerunds and infinitives.

E. Go online for the grammar expansion.

In this assignment, you are going to write an analysis essay using reasons and examples. As you prepare your essay, think about the Unit Question, "Why do people help each other?" Use information from Reading 1, Reading 2, the unit video, and your work in this unit to support your essay. Refer to the Self-Assessment checklist on page 156.

 Go to the Online Writing Tutor for a writing model and alternate Unit Assignments.

PLAN AND WRITE

A. BRAINSTORM Follow these steps to help you organize your ideas.

1. In a group, brainstorm reasons that might affect a person's decision to help others.

2. Brainstorm examples for your reasons in Step 1. Think about example situations or personal observations you can use to make your reasons clearer.

_____

_____

3. Think about the readings and video in this unit. Is there any information that can help support your ideas?

B. PLAN Follow these steps to plan your essay.

1. Write a thesis statement.

_____

_____

 2. Go to the Online Resources to download and complete the outline for your analysis essay.

 C. WRITE Use your PLAN notes to write your essay. Go to *iQ Online* to use the Online Writing Tutor.

1. Write your analysis essay that explains why people help each other. Be sure to use reasons and examples to support your thesis statement.

2. Look at the Self-Assessment checklist on page 156 to guide your writing.

REVISE AND EDIT

A. PEER REVIEW Read your partner's essay. Then go online and use the Peer Review worksheet. Discuss the review with your partner.

B. REWRITE Based on your partner's review, revise and rewrite your essay.

C. EDIT Complete the Self-Assessment checklist as you prepare to write the final draft of your essay. Be prepared to hand in your work or discuss it in class.

SELF-ASSESSMENT		
Yes	No	
☐	☐	Does the introductory paragraph include a thesis statement?
☐	☐	Does the essay include body paragraphs for each reason?
☐	☐	Does the essay contain examples to support the reasons?
☐	☐	Is *because* used correctly to state reasons? Are commas used if necessary?
☐	☐	Are gerunds with *-ing* forms used correctly?
☐	☐	Are all gerund subjects followed by a singular verb?
☐	☐	Does the essay contain phrasal verbs from the unit? Are they used correctly?
☐	☐	Does the essay include vocabulary from the unit?
☐	☐	Did you check the essay for grammar, punctuation, and spelling?

D. REFLECT Go to the Online Discussion Board to discuss these questions.

1. What is something new you learned in this unit?

2. Look back at the Unit Question—Why do people help each other? Is your answer different now than when you started the unit? If yes, how is it different? Why?

TRACK YOUR SUCCESS

Circle the words and phrases you have learned in this unit.

Nouns
factor 🔑 AWL
responsibility 🔑
subject 🔑
theory 🔑 AWL
witness 🔑

Verbs
hypothesize AWL
prove 🔑

Phrasal Verbs
apply to 🔑
bring about

call out
end up
figure out
grow out of
help out
point out
rely on 🔑 AWL
set up
watch out

Adjectives
altruistic
compassionate

complex 🔑 AWL
initial 🔑 AWL

Adverb
barely 🔑

Phrase
according to 🔑

🔑 Oxford 3000™ words
AWL Academic Word List

Check (✓) the skills you learned. If you need more work on a skill, refer to the page(s) in parentheses.

READING ☐	I can use a graphic organizer. (p. 140)
VOCABULARY ☐	I can use phrasal verbs. (p. 147)
WRITING ☐	I can state reasons and give examples. (p. 149)
GRAMMAR ☐	I can use gerunds and infinitives. (p. 153)

 **UNIT OBJECTIVE** ☐ I can gather information and ideas to write an analysis essay about why people help each other.

UNIT 7

Economics

READING ▶ using a timeline
VOCABULARY ▶ collocations with nouns
WRITING ▶ writing a cause/effect essay
GRAMMAR ▶ complex sentences

UNIT QUESTION

How can a small amount of money make a big difference?

A Discuss these questions with your classmates.

1. Have you ever given money to help someone or an organization? How did it make you feel?

2. What kinds of organizations typically ask for money? How is the money used?

3. Look at the photo. What do you think is happening?

B Listen to *The Q Classroom* online. Then answer these questions.

1. Felix says that something small in one part of the world could be big in another. Do you agree? Do you think that your small donation could be something big to someone else?

2. Yuna says that even a small amount of money could make a big difference in someone's life. Can you think of examples of what kinds of things might make a big difference, but not cost very much?

C Go to the Online Discussion Board to discuss the Unit Question with your classmates.

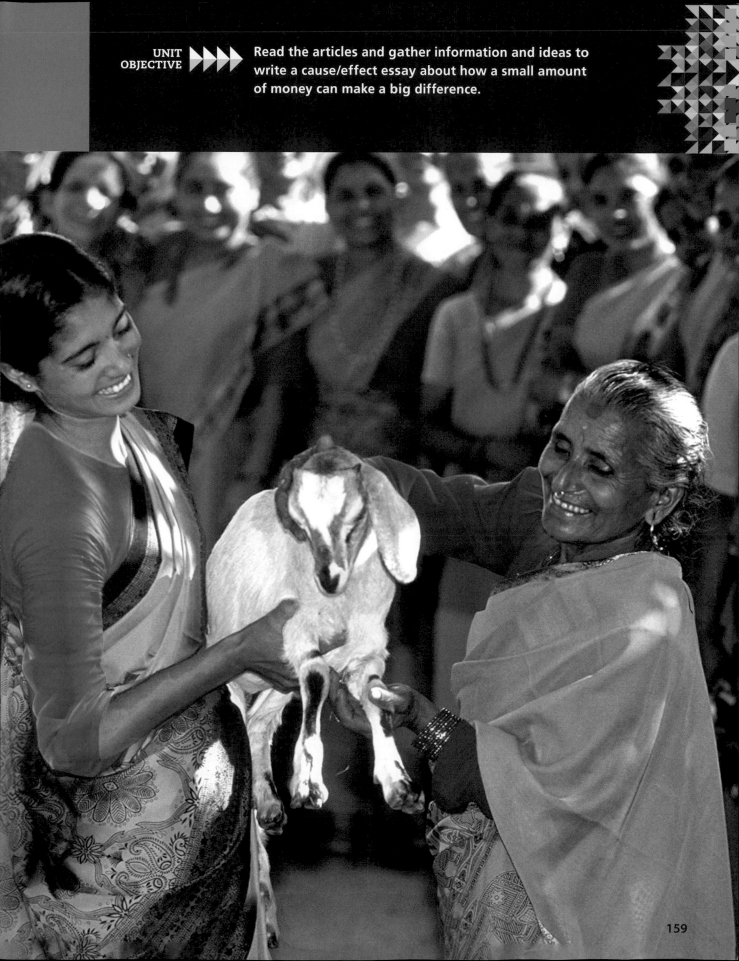

D The pictures show things that don't cost a lot of money, but they can have very positive results. What do you think these results might be? Match the pictures with the results.

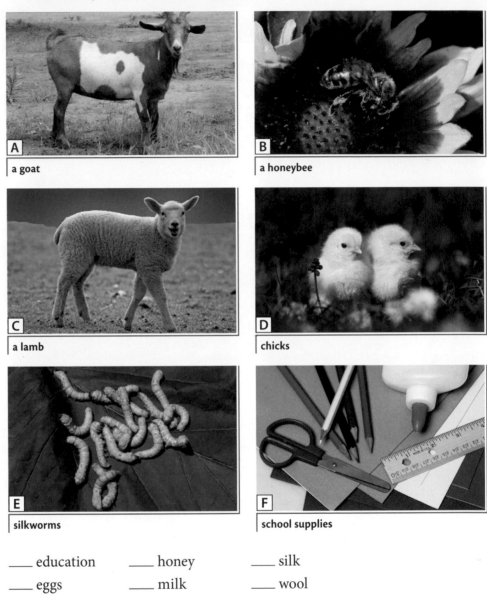

A a goat

B a honeybee

C a lamb

D chicks

E silkworms

F school supplies

| ___ education | ___ honey | ___ silk |
| ___ eggs | ___ milk | ___ wool |

E Read the saying. Then discuss the questions with a partner.

> Give a man a fish, and you feed him for a day. Teach a man to fish, and you feed him for a lifetime.

What do you think this saying means? How do you think the things in Activity D might relate to the saying?

READING

READING 1 | How a Ugandan Girl Got an Education

You are going to read an article about how a girl from a very poor village in Uganda became a college graduate with the help of people who donated to an organization. Use the article to gather information and ideas for your Unit Assignment.

PREVIEW THE READING

A. **PREVIEW** Read the first and last paragraphs. What kind of help do you think this girl received? Check (✓) your answers.

- ☐ money
- ☐ clothing
- ☐ food
- ☐ a tutor
- ☐ books
- ☐ an animal

B. **QUICK WRITE** Think about a time when you donated money or material goods, such as clothing or books. Write for 5–10 minutes in response. Be sure to use this section for your Unit Assignment.

C. **VOCABULARY** Check (✓) the words you know. Then work with a partner to locate each word in the reading. Use clues to help define the words you don't know. Check your definitions in the dictionary.

adjustment *(n.)*	generosity *(n.)*
attend *(v.)* 🔑	inspire *(v.)*
commitment *(n.)* 🔑	owe *(v.)* 🔑
distribute *(v.)* 🔑	proud *(adj.)* 🔑
extremely *(adv.)* 🔑	transition *(n.)* 🔑

🔑 Oxford 3000™ words

 D. Go online to listen and practice your pronunciation.

WORK WITH THE READING

⟫ **A.** Read the article and gather information about how a small amount of money can make a big difference.

How a Ugandan Girl Got an Education

1   Among the **proud** students receiving diplomas[1] at the 2008 graduation ceremony at Connecticut College was a young woman from Uganda named Beatrice Biira. And what makes her accomplishment so special is that she **owes** it all to a goat.

2   Beatrice grew up in the village of Kisinga in the mountains of Uganda. It is an **extremely** poor village, and Beatrice, the second oldest of six children, wanted very much to **attend** school, but her family didn't have the money to pay for it. In fact, the family was so poor that there was often not enough to eat. The only clothing Beatrice owned was a red dress that was cut open in the back so that she could grow into it.

3   All of this changed in 1993, when Beatrice was 9 years old, and her mother told her that, through the **generosity** of an organization named Heifer, they had received a goat. A goat? At the time, Beatrice could not see the value of something like a goat, especially when her mother told her that she would be responsible for caring for the goat.

4   Heifer International is a charity based in Little Rock, Arkansas which raises money to send animals to people in very poor countries. Its goal is to help people to become self-sufficient[2] by providing them with the animals and the education needed to care for them. The people receiving their help have to make the **commitment** to pass the gift on to others. Beatrice's mother and others in her village had applied to Heifer to receive help. The help came in the form of 12 goats that were **distributed** to the people in their village. Beatrice's family received one of these goats.

5   They named the goat Mugisa, which in Lokonzo, Beatrice's language, means "luck." And soon Beatrice realized how her luck would change because of this goat. Mugisa was pregnant when she came to Beatrice's family and soon gave birth to two more goats. The milk from the goats helped Beatrice and her siblings to get healthier, and they were soon able to

---

[1] **diploma:** the official piece of paper that shows you have completed a course of study

[2] **self-sufficient:** able to produce everything that you need without help from or having to buy from others

sell the additional milk. The family earned enough money to send Beatrice to school.

6   Though Beatrice was much older than the other children in school, she didn't mind. She breezed through the early grades as an excellent student. One day in 1995 a study tour, sponsored by Heifer, came to visit Beatrice's village. Two women who accompanied the tour, Page McBrier and Lori Lohstoeter, were impressed by Beatrice's passion for learning. They were **inspired** by her story and decided to write a children's book about her. They called it *Beatrice's Goat*.

7   Beatrice continued to be an excellent student and won a scholarship³ to a high school in Kampala, the capital of Uganda. While Beatrice was a student there in 2001, *Beatrice's Goat* was published and became a very popular *New York Times* bestseller. Beatrice was asked by Heifer to go on a book tour to the United States. While on this trip, she met a woman, Rosalee Sinn, who would become a great help to her. Ms. Sinn

and others helped her obtain a full scholarship to attend the Northfield Mount Hermon School in Massachusetts, a private preparatory school that had a program to help international students make the **transition** to college. For Beatrice, perhaps the biggest **adjustment** was the weather. She had never experienced cold weather before.

8   Despite the adjustments, Beatrice did very well at Northfield Mount Hermon, and while she was there, she applied to 11 colleges. She was accepted to half a dozen colleges, including some very prestigious ones. She decided to go to Connecticut College, where she won a scholarship. At first she wanted to become a veterinarian, but she soon decided to study economics and international studies. She wants to return to Uganda one day and use what she has learned to help her countrymen.

9   So in June 2008, there stood Beatrice in her cap and gown. This once very poor little girl from one of the poorest villages in the world was now a college graduate—all because of a goat!

---

³ **scholarship:** an amount of money that is given to a student to help them pay for their education

Vocabulary Skill Review

In Unit 6, you learned about phrasal verbs. Look carefully through Reading 1 again and underline examples of phrasal verbs. Look up the meaning in your dictionary.

B. **VOCABULARY** Here are some words from Reading 1. Read the sentences. Then write each bold word next to the correct definition on page 164.

1. Majda's parents were very **proud** of her for graduating with honors.

2. John is graduating from college soon. Yesterday he said, "I **owe** it all to my parents. Without their support, I couldn't have done it."

3. Mr. Buffett, the man who donated the money, is **extremely** rich and enjoys sharing his wealth.

4. Because of her good grades and leadership activities, Sara was able to **attend** the college she wanted.

5. When I arrived in the United States, my cousin provided me with a home, food, and money until I was able to find a job. I'm very grateful for her **generosity**.

6. When his parents agreed to pay for his education, Juan made a **commitment** to them that he would finish college.

7. The relief organization is collecting food and supplies, which it will **distribute** to victims of the earthquake.

8. When Carl meets his sister's students, it might **inspire** him to become a teacher, too.

9. Getting a part-time job at college is a good way to prepare yourself for the **transition** from school to the workforce.

10. Moving to England was a big **adjustment** for Fatima. She had to learn English and get used to cold weather.

a. _____ (*v.*) to give things to a number of people

b. _____ (*v.*) to exist or be successful because of someone or something

c. _____ (*n.*) a state of getting used to new conditions or a new situation

d. _____ (*adj.*) pleased and satisfied because you or someone you are close to has done something good

e. _____ (*n.*) the quality of giving more help or money than is usual or necessary

f. _____ (*v.*) to give a feeling of wanting and being able to do something good

g. _____ (*adv.*) very

h. _____ (*v.*) to go to or be present at a place

i. _____ (*n.*) something you have promised to do; a responsibility

j. _____ (*n.*) a change from one condition or form to another

volunteers unpacking supplies

 C. Go online for more practice with the vocabulary.

D. Read the sentences that contain the main idea of the paragraphs. Write the correct paragraph number before each sentence.

___ 1. Beatrice grew up in Uganda in a very poor family.

___ 2. Heifer International helps people by giving them animals and teaching them how to care for them.

___ 3. Beatrice's studies continued as she received scholarships to high school and a preparatory school.

___ 4. As a result of receiving a goat, Beatrice's family had enough money to send her to school.

___ 5. Beatrice was able to continue her education after her acceptance to many colleges.

___ 6. Beatrice's ability to learn quickly impressed some visitors to Kisinga.

E. Look at the main ideas that you identified in Activity D. Write the letter of the detail under the corresponding main idea. Main ideas 1, 3, 4, and 5 have two details each.

1. **Main idea:** Beatrice grew up in a very poor family.

   Details: _c_ , ____

2. **Main idea:** Heifer International helps people by giving them animals.

   Detail: ____

3. **Main idea:** Beatrice received scholarships to high school and a preparatory school.

   Details: ____ , ____

4. **Main idea:** After receiving a goat, Beatrice could go to school.

   Details: ____ , ____

5. **Main idea:** Beatrice continued her education in college.

   Details: ____ , ____

6. **Main idea:** Her ability to learn quickly impressed visitors.

   Detail: ____

a. McBrier and Lohstoeter wrote a book about her called *Beatrice's Goat.*

b. Beatrice went to Connecticut College on a scholarship.

c. Beatrice only had one dress.

d. Beatrice's mother had applied for help.

e. Beatrice won a scholarship to a high school in Kampala.

f. There was often not enough to eat.

g. The goat produced milk.

h. Beatrice was accepted to six colleges.

i. Beatrice's family sold the goat's milk.

j. Beatrice obtained a scholarship to Northfield Mount Hermon School.

F. Read the statements. Write *T* (true) or *F* (false). Then correct each false statement to make it true.

_____ 1.   Beatrice was happy when she learned about receiving a goat.

_____ 2.   Beatrice's mother had applied to an organization to get help.

_____ 3.   Beatrice's family soon had three goats.

_____ 4.   Beatrice had trouble learning in school because she was so much younger than the other children.

_____ 5.   Two women met Beatrice and decided to write a book about her, called *Beatrice's Story*.

_____ 6.   The biggest adjustment to studying in the United States for Beatrice was the food.

_____ 7.   She received a scholarship to go to a college in Connecticut.

_____ 8.   She graduated from college in 2008.

G. Go online to read *Teen Entrepreneurs* and check your comprehension.

WRITE WHAT YOU THINK

A. Discuss these questions in a group.

1.   Some good things happened after Beatrice's family received the goat: the goat produced milk, which helped make the family healthier, and the family sold the extra milk for money. What were some other benefits?

2.   Have you or someone you know ever donated to an organization that gives something directly to people in need? What was the organization? What did the receiver get from the donation?

3.   When people receive help from Heifer International, they have to agree to pass on the gift that they received. In Beatrice's case, her family had to pass on baby goats to another family in her village. How does this make the gift even bigger?

B. Choose one question and write a paragraph in response. Look back at your Quick Write on page 161 as you think about what you learned.

A **timeline** shows all of the important events that happened during a period of time. Timelines can be useful for understanding and remembering the events in a reading text. Look at the timeline for Reading 1, "How a Ugandan Girl Got an Education."

Beatrice's Life

1984	Beatrice was born.
1993	A goat was donated to Beatrice's family.
1995	A study tour sponsored by Heifer came to Beatrice's village.
2001	The book *Beatrice's Goat* was published.
2008	Beatrice graduated from Connecticut College.

A. Read the article. Then complete the timeline on page 168.

Tip for Success

A timeline is useful when reading a text in which many events occur. You can make a timeline as you're reading the text and then refer to it later.

From Salad Dressing to Summer Camp

Did you know that spending a few dollars on a bottle of salad dressing could help children with serious illnesses enjoy a week at summer camp? It's true, thanks to Newman's Own.

In December 1980, Paul Newman, a well-known American actor, and his friend A. E. Hotchner made gallons of salad dressing to give to family and friends as gifts. Their friends loved it and wanted more, so Hotchner and Newman made more. But this time they decided to sell the rest, and Newman's Own was born.

By the end of 1982, the first year of production, profits were close to $400,000. Since neither Newman nor Hotchner needed money, Newman said, "Let's give it all away to those who need it." Over the years, Newman's Own added more and more products. By the end of 2008, more than 40 products were being sold, and all of the profits went to charity, more than $265 million worth as of April 2009.

The profits have been donated to various charities, but the one closest to Newman's heart was the Hole in the Wall Gang camp, founded in 1988. This special camp is for seriously ill children. For one week, children at this camp can forget about their illnesses and enjoy themselves. Medical needs are taken care of, and since they are all sick, the children don't have to feel "different." It's all paid for through people buying salad dressing—a small price for such a great reward.

The Hole in the Wall Gang camp is founded.

Newman and Hotchner bottle salad dressing for gifts.

More than 40 Newman's Own products are sold.

Profits are close to $400,000.

History of Newman's Own

1980 ―――

1982 ―――

1988 ―――

2008 ―――

 B. Go online for more practice using a timeline.

READING 2 | # How to Make the Biggest Difference When Giving to Charity

 You are going to read an article about how donating just a small amount of money can help improve people's lives. Use the article to gather information and ideas for your Unit Assignment.

PREVIEW THE READING

A. PREVIEW Read the title and first paragraph. What kind of advice do you think this article is going to give?

☐ how to save money

☐ which charities are the best

☐ how much money you should give to charities

B. QUICK WRITE Think about a time when you wanted to help others, but you didn't have much money to donate. What did you do? Write for 5–10 minutes in response. Be sure to use this section for your Unit Assignment.

C. VOCABULARY Check (✓) the words you already know in the box on page 169. Use a dictionary to define any new or unknown words. Then discuss how the words will relate to the unit with a partner.

aim *(v.)* 🔑	**encourage** *(v.)* 🔑
ambition *(n.)* 🔑	**expand** *(v.)* 🔑
approach *(n.)* 🔑	**impact** *(n.)* 🔑
assumption *(n.)*	**measurable** *(adj.)*
enable *(v.)* 🔑	**network** *(n.)* 🔑

🔑 Oxford 3000™ words

 D. Go online to listen and practice your pronunciation.

WORK WITH THE READING

A. Read the article and gather information about how a small amount of money can make a big difference.

How to Make the Biggest Difference When Giving to Charity

Even if you only have a little money to give, you can still make big changes. Here's how small donations are improving lives in developing countries.

1   Before most of us learned to talk, we learned to share. It's a lesson we learned from parents at home, teachers in the lunchroom, and friends on the playground. Now we're all grown up, and we earn our own lunch money. Sharing is both easier and more difficult than it was when we were kids. We are in charge of our own money and possessions. We probably have more of them, yet so many organizations want our money. But it's time-consuming and confusing to figure out who will do the most with what we give.

2   Knowing how to give effectively is important to a responsible citizen with a desire to change the world. Those of us who are fortunate enough to have spare pennies can donate them. We don't need a great deal of wealth to be charitable. A number of great systems exist to help us. They can stretch our modest contributions, build philanthropic[1] **networks**, and fundraise successfully from numerous small donations. Remember, it's not the size of the donation that counts. It's how you use it.

3   While there are many opportunities to support important causes, there's usually very little opportunity to see our money have **measurable** effects on the people we wish to help. This is especially true when we only have a small amount to give. But there is a way for us to turn the least amount of money into the largest measurable effect over time. There is a type of giving that multiplies itself.

4   This **approach** can be called "enabling philanthropy." This is a virtuous[2] action that **enables** someone else to take a virtuous action, like giving someone a small loan, called a microloan, to start a small business

---

[1] **philanthropic:** helping the poor and those in need, especially by giving money

[2] **virtuous:** behaving in a moral or good way

that will eventually provide for all of his or her needs. We don't have to give annual checks to organizations and hope that our money has actually done some good. We can take a relatively small amount of money and **aim** it at the precise point where it can do maximum good. We can give this money not as charity, but as an investment in the **ambitions** of poor people in villages and cities. There is one condition for receiving this investment. The recipients[3] need to magnify this seed by starting a small business or enlarging an existing one. In addition, we can strongly **encourage** them to take some small portion of their growing investment to help someone else as well.

5   This is a virtuous circle that keeps on giving, paying its benefits forward generation after generation. It's a beautiful thing, and it's the only type of love you can hand out with money. There is also an optimistic **assumption** in this scheme. The two billion poorest people in the world are really two billion entrepreneurs just waiting for their first seed money. If you give it, they will build upon it.

6   As you look for opportunities to start your own virtuous circles, keep in mind the following important guidelines:

- Aim your gift at those with the least resources, to whom small amounts make a huge difference.

- Give at least $200. Though it may seem like a small amount, it's enough to make a real **impact** on the poorest recipients and to allow them to focus on their dreams of tomorrow. If you give less than that, the money can only help with immediate needs.

- Ask yourself if the gift will be able to **expand** itself, growing with each cycle.

- Focus your efforts on gifts that have a global range.

- Make sure that the agency that handles your donation sends the funds directly to individuals. The more steps between your donation and the recipient, the less impact it will have.

7   The following three organizations are highly successful programs that produce amazing results. Giving to these organizations will go far to make you optimistic about the world's future.

Heifer International: For 50 years, the Heifer Project has been providing families in developing countries (and in areas of the United States) with animals: cows, goats, pigs, rabbits, water buffalo, ducks, and so on. In the world's poorest regions, the cost of a cow or goat can exceed a year's income. This prevents many families from acquiring animals. When a family receives animals, they get meat, milk, or eggs. But more importantly, they get a source of income. They can sell the offspring. Each recipient must agree to give away one pair of offspring to another family. This is called passing on the gift. So a small contribution can multiply as families gain food, a source of income, the ability to help someone else—and pride. It's hard to imagine a better gift or a more practical, proven tool for making a difference in poor communities.

Opportunity International: Microfinancing is very popular in international circles. Tiny loans are made to workers in developing countries and the money is paid back very quickly. It's easy to contribute funds to a wide variety of microloan programs through Opportunity International. This organization has been providing microloans for 30 years. It works through Trust Banks, which are groups of 20 to 30 (mostly women) borrowers. The borrowers meet weekly to guarantee the loans.

Trickle Up: Trickle Up does not give out loans, but provides grants (typically $200) as seed money for people hoping to start small businesses— with strings attached. The recipients get some start-up cash and a lot of training. Trickle Up

---

[3] **recipient:** a person who receives something

makes grants to those looking to open small businesses like food stalls or repair shops. Those receiving the grants must agree to participate in basic business training and commit a minimum of 250 hours to their business in the first three months. They must also agree to reinvest at least 20 percent back into their business and keep an account ledger. That means that when you contribute to Trickle Up, you are building up a social network of new entrepreneurs.

some women training with Trickle Up

B. **VOCABULARY** Complete the paragraph with the vocabulary from Reading 2. You may need to change the form of the word to make the paragraph grammatically correct.

| aim *(v.)* | approach *(n.)* | enable *(v.)* | expand *(v.)* | measurable *(adj.)* |
| ambition *(n.)* | assumption *(n.)* | encourage *(v.)* | impact *(n.)* | network *(n.)* |

When I was in college, I decided to start a nonprofit organization to help people in need in my neighborhood. There were many people in need in the area where my college was located, and I had gotten to know a few of them, so my _____ was to use my background in economics to help them. My _____ was very simple: I tried to collect unwanted items from individuals and businesses. I worked with a(n) _____ of businesses in the area, both small and big. Working with these businesses _____ me to get donations of computers, books, and office supplies, as well as clothing and furniture. Every Saturday I set up a market in an empty building for people to purchase the goods. With the money I earned, I was able to purchase items needed for start-up businesses. I wanted to _____ people to follow their dreams, and in the process, to have a source of income. My first recipient was a single mother who made beautiful clothes in her home. With the money I loaned her, she was able to purchase a sewing machine and _____ her business. Soon she was selling her hand-made clothes on the Internet.

I tried to _____ my assistance at those who most needed it.

The _____ I had on the neighborhood was not only amazing,

but also _____. There were eight new businesses that started,

thanks to my donations. I worked under the _____ that

people are not poor by choice, and if given the opportunity to provide

for themselves, they would jump at the chance.

iQ ONLINE **C.** Go online for more practice with the vocabulary.

D. Complete the main ideas from Reading 2. Use the phrases in the box.

Heifer International	it keeps growing	a small amount
the impact	Opportunity International	someone's future or ambitions
in the right way	several guidelines	Trickle Up

1. It's hard to know which organization to give money to, but you still can

   donate _____ to do good, if it's used

   _____.

2. There is a way to see _____ of the money

   you give.

3. "Enabling philanthropy" is an investment in _____

   _____.

4. We need to look at this type of giving differently because _____

   _____.

5. There are _____ for giving.

6. _____ gives people a source of income that

   they can pass on.

7. _____ gives small loans to borrowers.

8. _____ gives seed money for small businesses.

E. Read the descriptions in the chart. Check (✓) the descriptions that apply to each organization.

	Heifer International	Opportunity International	Trickle Up
gives grants			✓
provides loans			
provides animals			
provides training			
asks for commitment			
gift expands			

F. According to the authors, which statements are true about giving to the types of charities described in the article? Check (✓) the true statements.

☐ A small amount of money, even $10, will help the recipients.

☐ You can see the effect on the recipients.

☐ You don't really know what effect your money has on the recipients.

☐ Your gift expands or multiplies.

☐ Your gift helps with someone's immediate needs, like food and clothing.

☐ Your gift helps the poorest people.

☐ Your gift may not go directly to the recipient.

☐ Your gift will provide a source of income.

☐ Your donation is aimed at exactly whom you want to help.

☐ Your gift is an investment in people.

☐ The recipients of your gift will be able to expand their business/income.

G. Complete the statements about Reading 2. Circle the correct answer.

1. In paragraph 1, line 9, the word *them* refers to ____.
   a. kids
   b. friends
   c. money
   d. money and possessions

2. In paragraph 2, line 7, the word *stretch* most likely means ____.
   a. make smaller
   b. make bigger
   c. receive
   d. give back

3. In paragraph 4, line 17, ***this seed*** refers to ___.
   a. a plant
   b. an investment
   c. a business
   d. an ambition

4. In paragraph 5, line 6, ***this scheme*** refers to ___.
   a. giving money away
   b. a new business
   c. a circle that keeps on giving
   d. taking money from others

5. In the section "Heifer International," the statement ***a cow or goat can exceed a year's income*** means ___.
   a. a cow or goat costs more than an annual salary
   b. an annual salary is more than the cost of a cow or goat
   c. a cow or goat is better than getting an annual salary
   d. a cow or goat can earn you an annual salary

WRITE WHAT YOU THINK

A. Discuss the questions in a group. Look back at your Quick Write on page 168 as you think about what you learned.

1. Have you ever given a small amount of money to a charity? If so, why did you donate? What was the purpose of the charity? If not, what kind of charity would you donate to? Why?

2. Have you ever donated to an organization that gives something directly to people in need? What was the organization? What did the recipient get from your donation?

B. Before you watch the video, discuss the questions in a group.

1. When you give a gift to someone, how do you feel? How does the other person feel?

2. How do you feel when you receive a gift from someone you know? How do you feel when the gift is from a stranger?

C. Go online to watch the video about how giving to others makes people happy. Then check your comprehension.

overextend *(v.)* to spend more money than you can manage without problems

pay it forward *(phr. v.)* to do something nice for someone

sustain *(v.)* to cause something to continue for a long period of time

D. Think about the unit video, Reading 1, and Reading 2 as you discuss the questions. Then choose one question and write a paragraph in response.

1. Both readings are about giving a small gift to others. The effect of this giving is positive for both the giver and the receiver. Who do you think benefits more? Why?

2. Do you think giving to an organization like Heifer International is better in the long run than giving to other more established charities? Why or why not? Do you think the impact of your giving is the same?

3. There's a saying, "It's better to give than to receive." Do you think this saying is true? Do you feel happy when you give to others? Why or why not?

Vocabulary Skill | Collocations with nouns

Collocations are words that are frequently used together. Learning collocations can improve your vocabulary and can help your writing sound more natural. Look at these examples of collocations.

> <u>Through the generosity</u> of an organization named Heifer, Beatrice's family received a goat.
> During the semester, the professor asks students to do five small <u>acts of kindness</u> a day.

Read the list of collocations that use the nouns *generosity* and *kindness*.

through the generosity of (someone): because of the donations (money) or kindness of (someone)

extraordinary generosity: the quality of being willing to give, or the act of giving an unusual amount of time or money

generosity toward (someone): unselfish actions that help someone

an act of kindness: a small action to help someone

treat (someone) with kindness: to behave in a compassionate way toward someone

the kindness of strangers: help from people you don't know

A. Read the paragraph. Underline the collocations from the Vocabulary Skill box on page 175.

Unexpected Help

In May 2008, a very strong tornado raced through a small town in the plains of Kansas. As a result, the home of the Milano family was completely destroyed. They lost everything they owned. But a remarkable thing happened after the storm passed. The town came together and showed extraordinary generosity. Someone offered them a place to live. Many families came to offer food, clothing, and things like blankets and pillows. The Milanos were treated with kindness by their neighbors. Through the generosity of a wealthy businessman, the Milanos had enough money to begin to rebuild their home. Mrs. Milano was amazed at the kindness of strangers; people she had never met sent checks and clothing from miles away. But perhaps the biggest act of kindness came from a young boy who gave his bicycle to the youngest Milano child.

B. Choose three collocations from the Skill Box on page 175. Write a sentence using each collocation.

1. _____

   _____

2. _____

   _____

3. _____

   _____

iQ ONLINE   **C.** Go online for more practice with noun collocations.

WRITING

UNIT OBJECTIVE ▶▶▶▶ At the end of this unit, you will write a cause/effect essay about how a small amount of money can make a big difference. This essay will include specific information from the readings and your own ideas.

Writing Skill | Writing a cause/effect essay

A **cause/effect essay** analyzes the causes (reasons) and effects (results) of a situation or event. A cause/effect essay includes an introductory paragraph, body paragraphs, and a concluding paragraph.

In a cause/effect essay, the introductory paragraph describes the situation or cause, gives background information, and includes a thesis statement (main idea). The thesis statement in a cause/effect essay describes the effects of the situation.

The body paragraphs of an essay provide support for the thesis statement. In a cause/effect essay, each body paragraph includes a topic sentence that states a supporting point and describes an effect. Other sentences in a body paragraph provide examples, details, or facts.

In a cause/effect essay, the concluding paragraph restates the main idea and often offers some additional thoughts or predictions for the future.

A. WRITING MODEL Read the model cause/effect essay. Underline the thesis statement.

My Friend Bill

In one of my college classes this semester, we were required to do an act of kindness for the elderly. My project involved buying food and preparing lunch for an elderly person. I spent about $10. The lunch included soup, a sandwich, and dessert. I packed up the lunch and went off to meet my new friend. A project like this one can result in new friendships, less loneliness, and the possible discovery of a career path! As a result of this project, I made a new friend and a lonely person was given the chance to share his life with someone again, but perhaps most importantly, I found a career path that interests me.

The person I visited was an 85-year-old man named Bill, who was unable to walk more than a few steps due to health issues. When I brought him the meal, he was very happy to see me. He has no family, and the only person he sees is the nurse's aide who comes every morning to help him get dressed and to give him his medicine. It was a treat for him to eat a meal with someone because he usually eats alone. He thought the food was great, but even more than the food, he enjoyed having someone to talk to.

Tip for Success

Cause/effect essays are common in almost every academic field of study from history to science to English. It's important to learn about this type of essay.

When I started talking to Bill, I found out that he had had a very interesting life. He had been a train engineer when train travel was much more popular. He had so many interesting stories to tell about his travels and adventures while working on the railroad. I really enjoyed talking to him, and it was especially interesting to me because I was planning a trip over the summer to see other parts of the country. I had been considering traveling by train, and after meeting Bill, I have no doubt in my mind that I will be going by train.

Perhaps the biggest effect of this project was that I realized that working with the elderly is an area that I'm very interested in. I found out that I enjoy spending time with older people; they have so much life experience to offer. I am a good listener, and older people sometimes just want someone to listen to them, so it seems like a perfect match. As a result, I plan on focusing my studies on the elderly.

What started out as just another assignment for my class resulted in much more than I expected. It's hard to know who was affected more by this project, Bill or me. I learned how easy it is to be a great help to someone else. The reward that I received was in knowing I had helped someone; but I also met a person whom I truly enjoyed talking to and spending time with. I plan to continue to bring lunch to Bill once a week, but it won't be as part of my class work. It will be because I genuinely enjoy his company, and I think he enjoys mine as well. Hopefully in the future, I will be able to work with the elderly so that I can help even more people like Bill.

B. Complete the graphic organizer with information from the essay in Activity A.

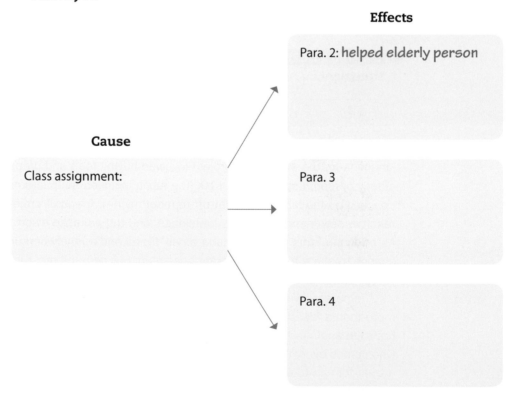

Effects

Para. 2: *helped elderly person*

Cause

Class assignment:

Para. 3

Para. 4

C. WRITING MODEL Read the model cause/effect essay. Then answer the questions.

Giving with TOMS Shoes

In 2006, Blake Mycoskie was traveling in South America and noticed that many children there had no shoes. A few months later, TOMS shoes was born. Mycoskie founded TOMS as a for-profit company that donates shoes to people around the world. The approach he uses is simple. He calls it "One for One." This means that for every pair of shoes that you buy, TOMS will donate a pair of shoes to someone in need. His company has done very well, and as of 2013, TOMS had given away over 10 million pairs of shoes. Owning a pair of new shoes may not seem like a really big deal to most of us. However, in many poor parts of the world, it *is* a big deal. Owning shoes can have a great impact on people's health, education, and well-being.

In many parts of the world, it is fairly common to see people, especially children, walking without shoes. However, there are many dangers to children when they do not wear shoes. In different parts of the world, many diseases, such as hookworm, can be contracted through the feet. Additionally, you can cut your feet on rough terrain or broken glass in some cases, which can lead to infection and risk of death. Finally, some climates are quite cold and the lack of footwear can lead to illness. So, simply owning a pair of shoes helps to maintain a child's health.

A second, and perhaps more important effect of owning a pair of shoes involves education. In many countries around the world, schools are not free. Parents must pay school fees and provide their children with uniforms, including shoes, in order for them to attend school. In some countries, children are not permitted to go to school if they don't have shoes. An additional benefit to owning a pair of shoes is that a child will be able to go to school.

Finally, when children receive new pairs of shoes, it makes them feel better about themselves. In many cases, this may be the first pair of shoes that the child has ever owned. It may even be the first *new* clothing the child has ever owned. In either situation, this improves a child's self-esteem. Children are thrilled to be able to walk through their villages in their new shoes. An increase in self-esteem is something that is not even measurable.

In conclusion, Mycoskie saw a need and established a company that is giving as much as it's getting in profits. So, when you purchase a pair of shoes from this company, you, too, are giving to the company. You're also getting back the satisfaction of knowing that someone else is benefiting in many ways from your purchase.

1. What is the situation or cause that is described in this essay?

_____

_____

2. Find the thesis statement of the essay. Write it below.

_____

_____

3. What is the effect or result in body paragraph 1? Write it below.

_____

4. Write down one detail or example that the writer uses to support the first effect.

_____

5. What is the effect or result in body paragraph 2? Write it below.

_____

6. Write down one detail or example that the writer uses to support the second effect.

_____

7. What is the effect or result in body paragraph 3? Write it below.

_____

8. Write down one detail or example that the writer uses to support the third effect.

_____

 **E. Go online for more practice with writing a cause/effect essay.**

Grammar | Complex sentences

 Tip for Success

Dependent clauses with *because*, *since*, and *when* are frequently used in cause/effect essays. The dependent clause with *because*, *since*, or *when* is the cause and the main clause is the effect.

A **complex sentence** has an independent clause, or main clause, and one or more dependent clauses. A **clause** is a group of words that has a subject and a verb. An independent clause can stand alone as a complete sentence. A dependent clause cannot stand alone and must be used with a main clause. Dependent clauses that show **cause** can begin with subordinators like *because*, *since*, and *when*. Look at these examples.

> Beatrice was not very happy **when** her mother told her about the goat.
> **Because** people in the United States donated money, her family received a goat.

The parts of the sentences beginning with *because* and *when* are dependent clauses. If a dependent clause comes before the main clause, it is followed by a comma.

> dependent clause ──────────────── main clause
> Because people in the United States donated money, her family received a goat.

A. Underline the dependent clauses.

1. Their new computer repair business grew in the first year <u>because they all worked night and day</u>.

2. Since there was very little rain all spring, the amount of corn grown was very small.

3. When he invested $300 in the new company many years ago, he didn't know how much money he would make.

4. The school can now pick up many more children because someone donated another school bus.

5. They were able to finish building the house in a week since many volunteers came to help.

B. Combine the sentences with the words in parentheses. Add a comma where necessary.

1. Sammy saved all of the money he made in his summer job. He finally had enough money to buy a car.
   (because)

   <u>Because Sammy saved all of the money he made in his summer job, he finally</u>

   <u>had enough money to buy a car.</u>

2. The village no longer floods. The villagers planted a hundred trees on the hillside.

(since)

_____

_____

3. The organization had received enough donations. It bought the new equipment.

(when)

_____

_____

4. Mr. Kelly donated a great deal of money to the children's fund. He knew that the children needed a new school.

(because)

_____

_____

5. People in the village suffered from extreme poverty. Many families could not afford to send their children to school.

(since)

_____

_____

C. Go online for more practice with complex sentences.

D. Go online for the grammar expansion.

 UNIT OBJECTIVE ▶▶▶▶ In this assignment, you are going to write a cause/effect essay. As you prepare your essay, think about the Unit Question, "How can a small amount of money make a big difference?" Use information from Reading 1, Reading 2, the unit video, and your work in this unit to support your essay. Refer to the Self-Assessment checklist on page 184.

iQ ONLINE Go to the Online Writing Tutor for a writing model and alternate Unit Assignments.

PLAN AND WRITE

 **Critical Thinking** Tip

The Brainstorm activity asks you to **participate** with your group. When you participate, you work with others to apply what you have learned to a new situation or problem. Active **participation** helps you remember information better.

A. BRAINSTORM Work in a group. Brainstorm situations in which a small amount of money can make a big difference.

B. PLAN Follow these steps to plan your essay.

1. Choose one of the situations from Activity A. Think of at least three effects or results of this situation. Complete the graphic organizer with your ideas.

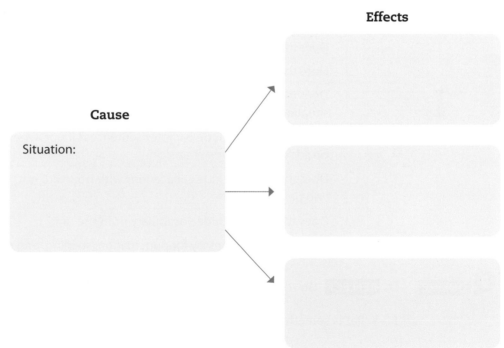

Effects

Cause

Situation:

2. Go to the Online Resources to download and complete the outline for your cause/effect essay.

C. **WRITE** Use your **PLAN** notes to write your essay. Go to *iQ Online* to use the Online Writing Tutor.

1. Write your cause/effect essay.

2. Look at the Self-Assessment checklist below to guide your writing.

REVISE AND EDIT

A. **PEER REVIEW** Read your partner's essay. Then go online and use the Peer Review worksheet. Discuss the review with your partner.

B. **REWRITE** Based on your partner's review, revise and rewrite your essay.

C. **EDIT** Complete the Self-Assessment checklist as you prepare to write the final draft of your essay. Be prepared to hand in your work or discuss it in class.

SELF-ASSESSMENT		
Yes	No	
☐	☐	Does the Introductory paragraph contain a thesis statement?
☐	☐	Does the introductory paragraph describe the situation (cause) and its effects?
☐	☐	Does the essay include three body paragraphs that each describe an effect?
☐	☐	Does the essay include a concluding paragraph that summarizes the situation (cause) and its effects?
☐	☐	Does the essay include complex sentences? If not, where could one or two be added?
☐	☐	Does the essay include collocations with nouns? If not, where could one or two be added?
☐	☐	Does the essay include vocabulary from the unit?
☐	☐	Did you check the essay for punctuation, spelling, and grammar?

D. **REFLECT** Go to the Online Discussion Board to discuss these questions.

1. What is something new you learned in this unit?

2. Look back at the Unit Question—How can a small amount of money make a big difference? Is your answer different now than when you started the unit? If yes, how is it different? Why?

TRACK YOUR SUCCESS

Circle the words and phrases you have learned in this unit.

Nouns
adjustment AWL
ambition 🔑
approach 🔑 AWL
assumption AWL
commitment 🔑 AWL
generosity
impact 🔑 AWL
network 🔑 AWL
transition 🔑

Verbs
aim 🔑
attend 🔑
distribute 🔑 AWL
enable 🔑 AWL
encourage 🔑
expand 🔑 AWL
inspire
owe 🔑

Adjectives
measurable
proud 🔑

Adverb
extremely 🔑

Collocations
an act of kindness
extraordinary
    generosity
generosity toward
    (someone)
the kindness of
    strangers
through the generosity
    of (someone)
treat (someone) with
    kindness

🔑 Oxford 3000™ words
AWL Academic Word List

Check (✓) the skills you learned. If you need more work on a skill, refer to the page(s) in parentheses.

READING	☐ I can use a timeline. (p. 167)
VOCABULARY	☐ I can use collocations with nouns. (p. 175)
WRITING	☐ I can write a cause/effect essay. (p. 177)
GRAMMAR	☐ I can use complex sentences. (p. 181)
UNIT OBJECTIVE 	☐ I can gather information and ideas to write a cause/effect essay about how a small amount of money can make a big difference.

READING ▶ scanning a text
VOCABULARY ▶ collocations with adjectives + prepositions
WRITING ▶ writing an argumentative essay
GRAMMAR ▶ sentence fragments

UNIT QUESTION

What does it take to be successful?

A Discuss these questions with your classmates.

1. How does someone become a successful athlete?

2. What are some things people give up or sacrifice in order to be successful?

3. Look at the photo. What do you think these people did to be successful?

UNIT
OBJECTIVE 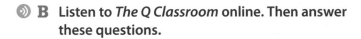 Read the articles and gather information and ideas to
write an argumentative essay about what it takes to be
successful.

B Listen to *The Q Classroom* online. Then answer
these questions.

1. Felix believes success does not have to be about
   money or a career. How can a person be successful
   without earning a lot of money?

2. Sophy believes that people can't be successful by
   themselves. Do you agree or disagree? Why?

3. Marcus states that people need to be able to adapt to changes in order
   to be successful. Do you feel the same way? Can you give an example?

iQ ONLINE
C Go online to watch the video about Major League Soccer in the
United States. Then check your comprehension.

VIDEO VOCABULARY

fanatic *(n.)* a person who is very
enthusiastic and excited about
something

hone *(v.)* to improve your skill at
doing something

league *(n.)* a group of sports clubs that
compete with each other for a prize

MLS *(abbr.)* Major League Soccer

scout *(n.)* a person whose job is to find
people who are good at sports, music,
etc., in order to give them jobs

iQ ONLINE
D Go to the Online Discussion Board to discuss the
Unit Question with your classmates.

187

E Read the statements. Check (✓) whether you agree or disagree with each statement. Discuss your answers with a partner.

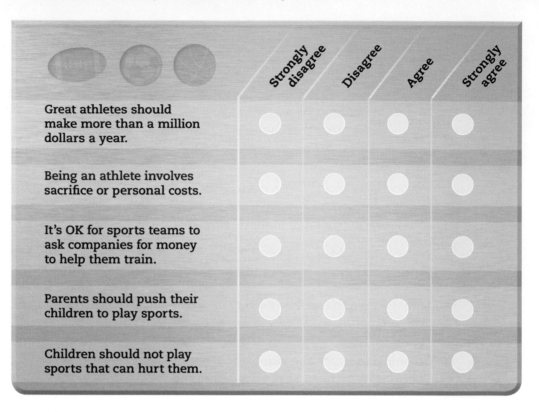

	Strongly disagree	Disagree	Agree	Strongly agree
Great athletes should make more than a million dollars a year.	○	○	○	○
Being an athlete involves sacrifice or personal costs.	○	○	○	○
It's OK for sports teams to ask companies for money to help them train.	○	○	○	○
Parents should push their children to play sports.	○	○	○	○
Children should not play sports that can hurt them.	○	○	○	○

Critical Thinking Tip

Activity F includes an idea map, which is a kind of diagram. When you **diagram** your ideas, you are analyzing how those ideas are connected to each other. Understanding those connections can help you speak and write more clearly.

F Write the name of your favorite sport in the idea map. Think about the costs or sacrifices someone needs to make in order to be successful at it. Write your ideas in the idea map. Then discuss your answers with your partner.

My Favorite Sport

Financial costs   Physical costs   Emotional costs

_____   _____   _____

_____   _____   _____

_____   _____   _____

READING 1 | Fast Cars, Big Money

 You are going to read an article from a business magazine about the popular sport of car racing from a business perspective. Use the article to gather information and ideas for your Unit Assignment.

PREVIEW THE READING

A. **PREVIEW** Read the headings. What do you think is the purpose of the article? Check (✓) your answer.

☐ to explain the sport of Formula 1 car racing

☐ to encourage businesses to invest in car racing

☐ to compare Formula 1 car races around the world

☐ to show why car racing is an expensive sport

B. **QUICK WRITE** What are some ways businesses attract more customers? Write for 5–10 minutes in response. Be sure to use this section for your Unit Assignment.

C. **VOCABULARY** Check (✓) the words you know. Then work with a partner to locate each word in the reading. Use clues to help define the words you don't know. Check your definitions in the dictionary.

assured *(adj.)*	**invest** *(v.)* 🔑	**profits** *(n.)* 🔑
dependable *(adj.)*	**logo** *(n.)*	**sponsor** *(v.)*
expansion *(n.)*	**market** *(n.)* 🔑	**stability** *(n.)*
image *(n.)* 🔑		

🔑 Oxford 3000™ words

 D. Go online to listen and practice your pronunciation.

Fast Cars, Big Money

Does your business need a boost?

1   Imagine 350 million people seeing your company **logo** every year. Imagine this number growing even higher every year. Imagine being part of one of the most prestigious[1] and glamorous[2] sports in the world and making millions of dollars at the same time. Sound attractive? Hundreds of companies have already discovered the financial benefits of **sponsoring** Formula 1 racing. When you choose to sponsor a team, you can be **assured** that your company will grow financially and globally.

Why are companies interested?

2   Companies have realized that investments in the sport of auto racing can bring them huge **profits**. Businesses, including banks, hotels, and telecommunication companies, **invest** tens of millions of dollars every year to sponsor race teams. Hundreds of millions of people watch car races every year. For companies, this is an enormous **market**.

3   Cars race around the track with company logos stuck to the doors, hood, and trunk, and people notice. Corporate sponsors can invest $5 million in a race team and make $30 million or more from car advertising. These costs are cheap compared to the profits. Sponsoring a team also shows the financial **stability** of your company. Race cars can cost tens of millions of dollars, and race teams can spend up to $300 million a year. Companies who invest in race teams are showing the world that they are powerful and **dependable**.

Why is investing now a good idea?

4   Much of Formula 1's current success comes from its **expansion** to global markets. Although most races are in Europe, today there are races in the Middle East and Asia. Companies support worldwide expansion because it gives them new customers in emerging markets. They can push their brand[3] globally. Many companies have already invested in Formula 1's most recent host locations, including Bahrain, Abu Dhabi, and Singapore. As a result, they have been able to expand their business to the Middle East and Asia. These areas of the world are full of

Formula 1 race car

---

[1] **prestigious:** respected or admired because of success
[2] **glamorous:** attractive or full of glamor

[3] **brand:** the name of a product that is made by a particular company

business opportunities, and Formula 1 racing has brought them more growth and success. Expanding overseas also shows that your company has a global message, which is important in today's global economy.

Why should my company invest?

5   Thanks to a strong business mentality, Formula 1 racing has become a profitable sport for corporations to invest in. The global economy is always changing, but the industry has succeeded by finding new ways to make more money. Sponsoring a team will not only bring your company profits, but will also improve your company's **image** as a business that is stable and global-minded. Take advantage of this wonderful business opportunity, and enjoy being part of this glamorous, thrill-seeking[4] sport. Vroom vroom!

[4] **thrill-seeking:** trying to find pleasure in excitement

B. **VOCABULARY** Here are some words from Reading 1. Read the sentences. Circle the word or phrase that can replace the bold word without changing the meaning of the sentence.

1. A company **logo** often gives the full name of the company or the first letter of the name. ((symbol) / address / rule)

2. Many companies regularly **sponsor** sports teams so that they can keep advertising on their uniforms. (support / watch / buy)

3. A brand-new business cannot be **assured** that it will succeed right away. (worried / sure / interested)

4. Businesses need to make **profits** consistently in order to be successful. (income / friends / decisions)

5. When companies **invest** money to make a new product, they have to consider the costs carefully. (need / lose / spend)

6. The Internet has given businesses access to a bigger **market** around the world. (number of customers / number of difficulties / number of computers)

7. Large companies generally have more **stability** than small businesses. (choice / strength / problems)

8. It is wise to invest in **dependable** companies because they tend to manage their money well. (new / reliable / different)

9. There has been a large **expansion** in the number of bilingual jobs because of the global economy. (decrease / growth / cost)

10. In order to be successful, a business needs to consider its **image**, or the way the public sees it. (attitude / appearance / growth)

D. Read the main ideas. Write the paragraph number where they are found.

__1__ 1. By sponsoring a Formula 1 team, a company will grow financially and globally.

____ 2. Formula 1 sponsorship is profitable and shows that a company is powerful and reliable.

____ 3. Sponsors can make a lot of money from car advertising.

____ 4. Formula 1 racing is a good investment today because of its expansion to global markets.

____ 5. Sponsorship brings companies profits and improves their image.

Writing

Activity F asks you to write a summary using the graphic organizer in Activity E. Use a graphic organizer before you write a summary to help you see how the ideas in a text are organized.

E. Work with a partner or group. Complete the graphic organizer for Reading 1. List two reasons that answer each question.

	Reason 1	Reason 2
1. Why are companies interested in Formula 1 racing?	Companies can make huge profits.	
2. Why is investing in Formula 1 racing now a good idea?		It shows your company has a global message.
3. Why should companies invest in Formula 1 racing?		

F. Write a summary of Reading 1. Use the graphic organizer in Activity E to help you write your summary.

Writing

Activity G asks you to identify what the words *this* and *these* refer to in a previous sentence. Writers use *this* and *these* to continue an idea in a following sentence. Use *this* for a singular noun. Use *these* for a plural noun.

G. Find these sentences in the article. Then answer the questions.

1. (Paragraph 1) Imagine **this** number growing even higher every year.

   What number does ***this*** refer to? _____

2. (Paragraph 2) For companies, **this** is an enormous market.

   What market does ***this*** refer to? _____

3. (Paragraph 3) **These** costs are cheap compared to the profits.

   What costs does ***these*** refer to? _____

4. (Paragraph 4) **These** areas of the world are full of business opportunities, and Formula 1 racing has brought them more growth and success.

What areas of the world does **these** refer to? _____

5. (Paragraph 5) Take advantage of **this** wonderful business opportunity, and enjoy being part of **this** glamorous, thrill-seeking sport.

   a. What business opportunity does **this** refer to? _____

   b. What sport does **this** refer to? _____

WRITE WHAT YOU THINK

A. Discuss these questions in a group.

1. Do you think sponsoring Formula 1 racing is a good or bad investment? Explain.

2. Do you think that businesses that sponsor sports like car racing would be as successful without giving sponsorship money? Why or why not?

3. Why do you think banks choose to advertise on Formula 1 racing cars?

B. Choose one question and write a paragraph in response. Look back at your Quick Write on page 189 as you think about what you learned.

Reading Skill	Scanning a text

Scanning means looking through a text quickly to find specific information, such as names, numbers, and dates. We scan items like the newspaper, a timetable, a dictionary, and the table of contents in a book. When you scan, do not read every word. Look for key words or phrases that will help you find the answer quickly. Think about how the information will appear on the page. For example, if you are looking for a date, scan only for numbers.

A. Scan Reading 1 for the missing information. Use key words in the sentences to help you find the answers. Then complete each statement.

1. Businesses that sponsor race teams include _____,

   _____, and _____.

2. Company logos are stuck to the _____, _____, and _____ of race cars.

3. Although most Formula 1 races are in Europe, today there are races in

   _____ and _____.

B. Scan Reading 1 again for the missing numbers. Use key words in the sentences to help you find the answers. Then complete each statement.

1. Every year, _____ million people watch Formula 1 races.

2. Businesses invest _____ of _____ of dollars every year to sponsor race teams.

3. Corporate sponsors can invest just _____ in a race team and make _____ or more.

4. Race teams can spend up to _____ a year.

 **C.** Go online for more practice scanning a text.

READING 2 | Practice Makes . . . Pain?

 You are going to read an article from an online newspaper about child athletes and what they do to succeed in sports. Use the article to gather information and ideas for your Unit Assignment.

PREVIEW THE READING

A. **PREVIEW** Look at the title. What do you think the writer will say about child athletes? Check (✓) your answer.

☐ It's easy for children to be successful in sports if they start early.

☐ The sacrifices children make for success in sports are sometimes too great.

Writing **Tip**

Remember to use reasons to explain the main idea in your topic sentence.

B. **QUICK WRITE** Are competitive sports good for children? Write for 5–10 minutes in response. Include a topic sentence and supporting details. Be sure to use this section for your Unit Assignment.

C. **VOCABULARY** Check (✓) the words you know. Then work with a partner to locate each word in the reading.

aggressively *(adv.)*	due to *(prep.)* 🔑	recover *(v.)* 🔑
dedication *(n.)*	exception *(n.)* 🔑	sign *(n.)* 🔑
demanding *(adj.)*	motion *(n.)* 🔑	trend *(n.)* 🔑

🔑 Oxford 3000™ words

 **D.** Go online to listen and practice your pronunciation.

Practice Makes . . . Pain?

1   At 10, Courtney Thompson was a top-ranked gymnast in New Hampshire. She had been doing flips since she was one and had her heart set on competing in the Olympics. She practiced four and a half hours a day, six days a week, often repeating the same move 100 times. Her **demanding** schedule took a toll[1]. It got to the point where Courtney could barely straighten her elbows unless she put ice on them. On January 12, 2005, she had to stop in the middle of a floor routine. "I jumped up and grabbed my arm. It hurt really bad."

2   Doctors discovered that Courtney's constant workouts had caused the cartilage, or connective tissue, in her elbow to separate from the bone. She had surgery on both arms and went through months of painful rehabilitation[2]. Courtney's experience is part of a growing **trend** in youth sports—kids and teens were starting to have the same type of injuries that only professional athletes used to have. Experts say kids are pushing their bodies to the limit, practicing sports too hard for too long. The exhausting schedules often lead to dangerous injuries that could keep young athletes from competing—permanently.

Under Strain

3   According to experts at *The Physician and Sportsmedicine* journal, between 30 and 50 percent of youth sports injuries are **due to** overuse. Overuse injuries are caused by repetitive **motion** that, over time, puts more stress on a body part than it can handle. The tissue or bone eventually breaks, stretches, or tears.

4   Danny Clark ended up with an overuse injury last year. The teen baseball player from Altamonte Springs, Florida hurt himself by throwing 80 pitches in a single game after two months of not pitching at all. The sudden repetitive action tore Danny's rotator cuff. The rotator cuff is a group of four muscles and the tendons that connect them to bones in the shoulder. Afterward, he couldn't pitch for two months and needed five months of physical therapy.

young baseball player

---

[1] **take a toll:** to have a negative effect

[2] **rehabilitation:** the process of returning to a normal life again after an injury

Too Much, Too Soon

5   Experts say injuries such as Danny's are on the rise, in part because more and more kids are leaving casual sports for organized team competitions that require hours of practice and game time. "Kids [are] playing sports more **aggressively** at younger ages," explains James Beaty, an orthopedist in Memphis, Tennessee.

6   Kevin Butcher, a 15-year-old soccer player from Fort Collins, Colorado, is no **exception**. He plays soccer three or four times a week for nine months a year. His **dedication** pays off—last year he helped lead his team to a state championship. But his success came with a price. "Last year, I sprained my ankle a few times, dislocated[3] a bone in my foot, and broke both sides of my pelvis[4]," Kevin says. The first time he broke his pelvis, Kevin didn't realize it for about a month. He played through the pain until doctors forced him to rest. When he dislocated a bone in his foot, a physical therapist put the bone into place, bandaged his foot, and let him play the next day.

children playing soccer

Knowing Your Limits

7   Not every kid who plays sports ends up with serious injuries. Experts say the key to avoiding injury is paying attention to your body. Feeling sore after practice is OK, but sharp pain is a warning **sign** that shouldn't be ignored. Kevin learned that lesson while **recovering** from his second broken pelvis in less than a year. "There's definitely a glory in playing through pain, but I think there is a limit. You just have to know when to stop."

---

[3] **dislocate:** to put a bone out of its correct position   [4] **pelvis:** the set of wide bones at the bottom of your back that connect to your legs

---

Vocabulary Skill Review

In Unit 4, you learned how to identify word forms with suffixes. Which of the vocabulary words in Activity B have a suffix making them a noun?

B. VOCABULARY **Here are some words from Reading 2. Read the sentences. Circle the answer that best matches the meaning of each bold word or phrase. Then compare your answers with a partner.**

1. Ice skating is a **demanding** sport that requires a lot of time, practice, and hard work.
   a. difficult   b. expensive   c. harmful

2. Putting kids in sports at a young age is a growing **trend** in many countries today.
   a. new profession   b. general change   c. high cost

3. We canceled the soccer game **due to** the pouring rain. It was too wet and dangerous to play.
   a. because of   b. in order to   c. late for

4. The official made a **motion** with his hand to let the runners know it was time to start the race.

   a. ticket   b. question   c. movement

5. Athletes who play sports **aggressively** get hurt more frequently than athletes who don't.

   a. forcefully   b. quietly   c. quickly

6. Most competitive athletes earn money for playing sports, but gymnasts are an **exception**. They do not receive a salary.

   a. new rule   b. someone not included   c. professional athlete

7. Competitive athletes must have **dedication** because it takes a lot of time and hard work to be successful in sports.

   a. money   b. skill   c. commitment

8. Sore, aching muscles are a warning **sign** that you have exercised very hard.

   a. signal   b. injury   c. sacrifice

9. It can take months for an athlete to **recover** from a serious injury.

   a. compete   b. get sick   c. get better

iQ ONLINE **C.** Go online for more practice with the vocabulary.

D. Answer the questions. Write the paragraph number where the answer is found. Then discuss your answers with a partner.

1. What are many youth sport injuries due to? Paragraph: ____

   _____

2. What causes an overuse injury? Paragraph: ____

   _____

3. Why do children in youth sports have more injuries today? Paragraph: ____

   _____

4. Why do organized team competitions cause more injuries? Paragraph: ____

   _____

5. How can child athletes avoid injury? Paragraph: ____

   _____

Tip for Success

Activity E asks you to complete a **chart**. A chart is a graphic organizer readers use to see relationships between ideas. Identifying relationships between ideas in a text will help you become a more effective reader.

E. Scan Reading 2. Complete the chart with the missing information.

	Name	Home	Sport	Injury
1.	Courtney Thompson	New Hampshire		
2.			baseball	
3.				sprained ankle, dislocated bone, broken pelvis

F. Read the statements. Write *F* (fact) or *O* (opinion).

_____ 1. Courtney Thompson practiced gymnastics six days a week.

_____ 2. Between 30 and 50 percent of youth sports injuries are due to overuse.

_____ 3. Overuse injuries are caused by physical stress on tissue or bone.

_____ 4. Child athletes are playing sports too hard for too long.

_____ 5. The number of overuse injuries in children is increasing.

_____ 6. Soccer player Kevin Butcher showed a lot of dedication.

_____ 7. Kevin Butcher's soccer team won the state championship last year.

_____ 8. Listening to your body is an important lesson for athletes to learn.

G. Check (✓) the statements you can infer from the reading.

☐ 1. Overuse injuries are usually permanent.

☐ 2. Fewer children had overuse injuries in the past.

☐ 3. Overuse injuries happen more often to soccer players than baseball players.

☐ 4. It can take children months to recover from an overuse injury.

☐ 5. Parents do not want their children to play casual sports anymore.

☐ 6. It is normal for child athletes to feel sore after they practice sports.

☐ 7. Sharp pain can be a warning sign of an overuse injury.

☐ 8. Young athletes are more at risk of injuring themselves than older athletes are.

H. Why do you think some athletes like to "push through their pain" instead of quitting? Write 5–8 sentences giving your opinion.

I. Go online to read *An Idea So Crazy It Works* and check your comprehension.

WRITE WHAT YOU THINK

A. Discuss the questions in a group. Look back at your Quick Write on page 194 as you think about what you learned.

1. Do you think competing in sports is good for young children? Explain.

2. Do you think coaches and parents have a responsibility to try to stop children from getting hurt while doing sports? Why or why not?

B. Think about the unit video, Reading 1, and Reading 2 as you discuss the questions. Then choose one question and write a paragraph in response.

1. What are some ways that athletes pay for success?

2. How do parents of child athletes pay for success? Consider financial, physical, and psychological costs in your response.

Vocabulary Skill	Collocations with adjectives + prepositions

Collocations are words that frequently go together. One common pattern for collocations is adjective + preposition.

Adjective	+	Preposition	Adjective	+	Preposition
interested		in	famous		for
due		to	upset		about

Learning collocations will help you increase your vocabulary and improve your writing.

A. Complete each sentence below with the correct adjective + preposition collocation.

afraid of	famous for	involved in	sure about
due to	interested in	nervous about	upset about

1. Parents whose children compete in sports are often __*afraid of*__ injuries.

2. The player's injury was _____ overuse.

3. Carlos was not _____ the meaning of the word, so he looked it up in the dictionary.

4. Felix was very _____ losing the championship game. He really wanted to win.

5. Nadia Comăneci is _____ being one of the greatest gymnasts in history.

6. More children are _____ organized sports at a very young age today. My neighbor's son started playing soccer when he was four.

7. Are you _____ going to the baseball game tonight? I have an extra ticket if you'd like to go.

8. The gymnast was _____ competing for the first time in front of hundreds of people.

B. Choose five adjective + preposition collocations from Activity A. Write a sentence using each collocation.

1. _____

_____

2. _____

_____

3. _____

_____

4. _____

_____

5. _____

_____

iQ ONLINE **C.** Go online for more practice using collocations with adjectives + prepositions.

WRITING

UNIT OBJECTIVE ▶▶▶▶ **At the end of this unit, you will write an argumentative essay about what it takes to be successful. This essay will include specific information from the readings and your own ideas.**

Writing Skill	Writing an argumentative essay

An **argumentative essay** expresses how you feel about a topic. For example, it might express whether you agree or disagree with an idea.

The introductory paragraph in an argumentative essay includes the thesis statement, which clearly states the writer's opinion or view about a topic. The introductory paragraph may include background information and a **counterargument** to the writer's opinion. A counterargument is the opposite opinion. Writers sometimes mention a counterargument and then explain why it's not true in order to make their point stronger.

Each body paragraph of an argumentative essay includes a topic sentence that states a reason for the writer's opinion. Examples or facts are given to support each reason.

The concluding paragraph of an argumentative essay restates the opinion and refers to the counterargument. The concluding paragraph also summarizes the reasons the writer has this opinion. Often, the concluding paragraph includes an additional idea, sometimes a prediction, about the topic.

Tip for Success

Writers use certain phrases to introduce a counterargument, such as *some people say that, some people think that,* and *some people argue that.*

A. **WRITING MODEL** **Read the model argumentative essay. Then answer the questions on pages 202–203.**

Competitive Soccer: An Ideal Sport for Children

Soccer is the most popular sport in the world, and for many people, it is an important part of their childhood. Many children join competitive soccer leagues at a very young age. Some parents, however, believe that competitive soccer is too dangerous. They worry about their children getting a serious injury, so they decide to put them in a less aggressive team sport like basketball or baseball. I don't think this is a good enough reason not to let children play soccer. The fact is that children can get injured playing any sport. Even baseball players can get serious injuries. If children aren't allowed to join competitive soccer leagues, I believe they will miss out on very important advantages of playing this wonderful sport. Soccer is an ideal sport for children, and as a competitive soccer player, a child will not only get a good physical workout, but will also learn valuable lessons about teamwork and discipline.

First, playing competitive soccer keeps children in good shape. Soccer players build strength, flexibility, and endurance. Unlike some sports, soccer requires children to move around constantly. This constant motion helps players build muscles and burn fat more efficiently. Running not only strengthens leg muscles, but also burns a lot of calories, and it improves heart health. Children who play less active competitive sports, like baseball, do not enjoy these same advantages because they can spend long stretches of time just standing around.

Second, being a competitive soccer player teaches children the importance of teamwork. A soccer team has 11 players and several positions. Forwards score goals, fullbacks and goalies defend, and halfbacks assist both forwards and fullbacks. All of these players depend on each other during a game. Therefore, they have to learn to communicate well and they must trust one another, if they want to win. Learning teamwork, good communication skills, and trust will not just help children succeed on a competitive soccer team—the truth is these skills and values will also be useful in their lives at home, at school, and eventually, into adulthood.

Finally, competitive soccer is one of the best ways for children to learn about discipline. Players often practice after school or early in the morning, and they have games during the weekend. Young soccer players, however, also have to worry about completing all their schoolwork. In order to do both successfully, children learn how to manage their time effectively to meet homework deadlines and to show up to soccer practice on time. Competitive players also have to take good care of themselves by eating healthy food and keeping their bodies in good shape, which teaches them self-control.

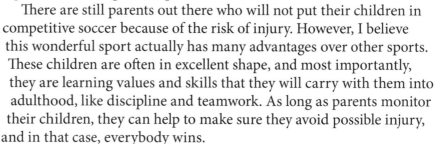

There are still parents out there who will not put their children in competitive soccer because of the risk of injury. However, I believe this wonderful sport actually has many advantages over other sports. These children are often in excellent shape, and most importantly, they are learning values and skills that they will carry with them into adulthood, like discipline and teamwork. As long as parents monitor their children, they can help to make sure they avoid possible injury, and in that case, everybody wins.

1. Look at the introductory paragraph. What is the counterargument? Circle it. Which sentence states the writer's opinion about the topic? Underline it.

2. Look at the body paragraphs. What are the three reasons that the writer gives for his or her opinion?

Reason 1: _____

_____

Reason 2: _____

_____

Reason 3: _____

_____

3. Look at the concluding paragraph. Which sentence refers to the counterargument? Circle it. Which sentence restates the writer's opinion? Underline it.

4. What additional idea does the writer include in the concluding paragraph? Why do you think the writer added this idea?

_____

_____

Tip for Success

Activity B asks you to give your opinion about something you've read. When you state whether you agree or disagree with an author, include reasons for your opinion so that your ideas are well supported.

B. Look again at the model essay in Activity A. Do you agree or disagree with the writer? Write 5–8 sentences giving your opinion. Include reasons to support your opinion.

C. WRITING MODEL Read the essay question. Then read the introductory paragraph and first body paragraph for an argumentative essay. Answer the questions on page 204.

Essay question: *Should parents let their child athletes leave home at an early age so they can train for the Olympics?*

Experts agree that child athletes are training harder and longer than they did in the past. Compared to before, children today who take up competitive sports, like figure skating or gymnastics, train so seriously that many leave home at a young age to follow their dream. In fact, gymnasts as young as eight years old may leave home and live far away to train with the best coaches. This is because many parents believe good coaches will give their children the opportunity to compete in the Olympics one day, and it is worth the sacrifice. However, I believe sending athletes away from home so young is not the right choice. Parents of these young competitive athletes should not let them leave home to train for the Olympics for three important reasons.

First of all, parents should not let their children leave home to train because they lose precious time with them. Children will not live with their parents forever. The years they spend with their parents go very quickly. One day they're in kindergarten, and the next day it seems like they're off to college. Sending children away may make them better athletes, but it cannot replace this lost time together. For example, they won't be able to read together every night or go shopping together whenever they want. Parents could also miss out on important events, like birthdays or the first day at a new school. I think parents will regret their decision when their children are grown up and they have missed these important days and events.

1. Circle the sentence in the introductory paragraph that states the counterargument.

2. Underline the sentence in the introductory paragraph that gives the writer's opinion about the topic.

3. What reason does the writer give to support his or her opinion? Circle the sentence in the body paragraph that states the reason.

4. The writer states, "Sending children away may make them better athletes, but it cannot replace **this lost time** together."

   What does *this lost time* refer to? _____

5. What examples does the writer use to support his or her reason in the body paragraph?

   Example 1: _not able to read together every night_____

   Example 2: _____

   Example 3: _____

   Example 4: _____

6. Do you think the writer's first reason is convincing? Why or why not? Share your answer with a partner.

Writing Tip

Activity D asks you to provide examples. Writers often use *for example* and *for instance* to signal examples. *For example* and *for instance* usually begin a new sentence and are followed by a comma.

D. Read the topic sentence for a second body paragraph for the essay assignment in Activity C. Write 5–8 supporting sentences for the paragraph. Include examples to support the reason in the topic sentence.

Second, parents who send their children to train far away from home will not be able to be around when their children need them. For example,

E. Read this concluding paragraph for the essay assignment in Activity C. Then answer the questions on page 205.

Many parents think letting their child athlete train far away from home is a good idea because it will help them compete in the Olympics one day. However, they also have to think about the consequences. I think parents will regret their decision later on because they will have missed out on important days and events in their children's lives, as well as moments when their children really needed them by their side. In addition, parents could be wasting their money, since only a small number of athletes make it to the Olympics, even if they show a lot of potential at a young age. For these three reasons, parents need to think very hard before making a decision that could negatively affect their lives and their children's lives for years to come.

1. Which sentence refers to the counterargument? Circle it.

2. Which sentence restates the writer's opinion and summarizes the first two reasons? Underline it.

3. According to the conclusion, what was the topic of the third body paragraph?

_____

_____

4. What prediction does the writer make at the end of the conclusion?

_____

_____

5. Do you agree or disagree with the writer's prediction? Why? Share your answer with a partner.

 F. Go online for more practice with writing an argumentative essay.

Grammar Sentence fragments

A **sentence fragment** is an incomplete sentence that cannot stand alone. Sentence fragments are usually considered errors. It is important to avoid sentence fragments in your writing. Look at the examples.

Fragment: When children play soccer.
Fragment: Because children can get injured.

As you learned in Unit 7, these examples are **dependent clauses**. When used alone, they are fragments. They need to be combined with a main clause.

<u>When children play soccer</u>, they learn the importance of teamwork.
Parents worry about competitive sports <u>because children can get injured</u>.

Words such as *because, since, although, when,* or *after* are often used with dependent clauses. These words connect an incomplete sentence to a main clause to avoid a fragment.

A. **Identify each sentence as a complete sentence (S) or a sentence fragment (F). Correct the sentence fragments with a partner.**

____ 1. When athletes feel pain.

____ 2. She always stretches for 20 minutes before she exercises.

____ 3. Because there are more children in competitive sports.

____ 4. Since I started playing soccer, I have lost weight.

____ 5. Although baseball looks easy to play.

B. **Read the paragraph and correct any fragments.**

> I loved playing basketball in high school because it helped me make a lot of new friends. When I was young. I was a very shy person. It was difficult for me to speak with people. Because I was so shy. Then a classmate invited me to try out for the basketball team. I was pretty good, and I was picked for the team. Although I was nervous at first. I really enjoyed working with my teammates. We were like a family. We supported each other. When we played together against other schools. Many of us became good friends off the court too. Little by little, I learned not to be so shy. Today I still keep in touch with my old teammates on social networking sites. Although we don't see each other anymore. We are still good friends. Thanks to them, I'm not shy like I used to be back in high school.

C. **Go online for more practice with sentence fragments.**

D. **Go online for the grammar expansion.**

 **Unit Assignment**   **Write an argumentative essay**

UNIT OBJECTIVE ▶▶▶▶   In this assignment, you are going to write an argumentative essay on one of the topics below. As you prepare your essay, think about the Unit Question, "What does it take to be successful?" Use information from Reading 1, Reading 2, the unit video, and your work in this unit to support your essay. Refer to the Self-Assessment checklist on page 208.

   Go to the Online Writing Tutor for a writing model and alternate Unit Assignments.

1. Should athletes or sports teams accept money from corporate sponsors in order to be successful? Discuss one or more specific sports in your essay.

2. Should child athletes be pushed hard in order to succeed? Discuss one or more specific sports in your essay.

PLAN AND WRITE

A. BRAINSTORM **Follow these steps to help you organize your ideas.**

1. Choose your topic. Then look at the list of sports. Check (✓) the sport or sports you would like to discuss in your essay.

☐ American football   ☐ rugby

☐ baseball   ☐ running

☐ basketball   ☐ soccer

☐ Formula 1 racing   ☐ tennis

☐ gymnastics   ☐ (other) _____

2. Brainstorm reasons that will help support your opinion about the topic.

3. Brainstorm a counterargument for your essay. Why would someone disagree with your opinion?

B. PLAN **Follow these steps to plan your essay.**

1. Write a thesis statement for your essay that expresses your opinion about the topic. List your three best reasons from Activity A.

   _____

   _____

   _____

   _____

2. Think about the readings and the video in this unit. Is there any information that can help support your ideas?

iQ ONLINE

3. Go to the Online Resources to download and complete the outline for your argumentative essay.

iQ ONLINE

C. WRITE **Use your** PLAN **notes to write your essay. Go to** *iQ Online* **to use the Online Writing Tutor.**

1. Write your argumentative essay that explains what it takes to be successful. Be sure to use reasons and examples or facts to support your thesis statement.

2. Look at the Self-Assessment checklist on page 208 to guide your writing.

REVISE AND EDIT

A. PEER REVIEW Read your partner's essay. Then go online and use the Peer Review worksheet. Discuss the review with your partner.

B. REWRITE Based on your partner's review, revise and rewrite your essay.

C. EDIT Complete the Self-Assessment checklist as you prepare to write the final draft of your essay. Be prepared to hand in your work or discuss it in class.

	SELF-ASSESSMENT	
Yes	**No**	
☐	☐	Does the essay include an introductory paragraph that states an opinion and describes a counterargument?
☐	☐	Does the essay include three body paragraphs that each provide a reason and supporting examples or facts?
☐	☐	Does the essay contain a concluding paragraph that restates the opinion, refers to the counterargument, and summarizes the reasons?
☐	☐	Are there any sentence fragments? Underline them and then correct them.
☐	☐	Are adjective + preposition collocations used correctly?
☐	☐	Does the essay include vocabulary from the unit?
☐	☐	Did you check the essay for punctuation, spelling, and grammar?

D. REFLECT Go to the Online Discussion Board to discuss these questions.

1. What is something new you learned in this unit?

2. Look back at the Unit Question—What does it take to be successful? Is your answer different now than when you started the unit? If yes, how is it different? Why?

TRACK YOUR SUCCESS

Circle the words and phrases you have learned in this unit.

Nouns
dedication
exception 🔑
expansion AWL
image 🔑 AWL
logo
market 🔑
motion 🔑
profits 🔑
sign 🔑
stability AWL
trend 🔑 AWL

Verbs
invest 🔑 AWL
recover 🔑 AWL
sponsor

Adjectives
assured AWL
demanding
dependable

Adverb
aggressively

Collocations
afraid of
due to 🔑
famous for
interested in
involved in 🔑
nervous about
sure about
upset about

🔑 Oxford 3000™ words
AWL Academic Word List

Check (✓) the skills you learned. If you need more work on a skill, refer to the page(s) in parentheses.

READING ☐ I can scan a text. (p. 193)
VOCABULARY ☐ I can use collocations with adjectives + prepositions. (p. 199)
WRITING ☐ I can write an argumentative essay (p. 201)
GRAMMAR ☐ I can recognize and avoid sentence fragments. (p. 205)

UNIT OBJECTIVE ▶▶▶▶ ☐ I can gather information and ideas to write an argumentative essay about what it takes to be successful.

AUTHORS AND CONSULTANTS

Authors

Margot F. Gramer holds an M.A. in TESOL from Teachers College, Columbia University. She has been involved in the field of ESL as a teacher, teacher-trainer, administrator, writer and editor. She has taught ESL for many years at both the college level and in business settings. She is the author or co-author of many ESL textbooks. She is currently an Instructor at the Language Immersion Program at Nassau Community College (LINCC) in Garden City, New York.

Colin S. Ward is Chair of the Languages Department at Lone Star College-North Harris in Houston, Texas. He holds an M.A. in TESOL from the University of London and has been teaching English for nearly fifteen years. His interests include the teaching of second-language writing and the role of technology in language learning. Colin is a U.S.-U.K. Fulbright scholar and the author of several ESL textbooks.

Series Consultants

ONLINE INTEGRATION

Chantal Hemmi holds an Ed.D. TEFL and is a Japan-based teacher trainer and curriculum designer. Since leaving her position as Academic Director of the British Council in Tokyo, she has been teaching at the Center for Language Education and Research at Sophia University on an EAP/CLIL program offered for undergraduates. She delivers lectures and teacher trainings throughout Japan, Indonesia, and Malaysia.

COMMUNICATIVE GRAMMAR

Nancy Schoenfeld holds an M.A. in TESOL from Biola University in La Mirada, California, and has been an English language instructor since 2000. She has taught ESL in California and Hawaii, and EFL in Thailand and Kuwait. She has also trained teachers in the United States and Indonesia. Her interests include teaching vocabulary, extensive reading, and student motivation. She is currently an English Language Instructor at Kuwait University.

WRITING

Marguerite Ann Snow holds a Ph.D. in Applied Linguistics from UCLA. She teaches in the TESOL M.A. program in the Charter College of Education at California State University, Los Angeles. She was a Fulbright scholar in Hong Kong and Cyprus. In 2006, she received the President's Distinguished Professor award at Cal State, LA. She has trained EFL teachers in Algeria, Argentina, Brazil, Egypt, Libya, Morocco, Pakistan, Peru, Spain, and Turkey. She is the author/editor of publications in the areas of integrated content, English for academic purposes, and standards for English teaching and learning. She recently served as a co-editor of *Teaching English as a Second or Foreign Language* (4th ed.).

VOCABULARY

Cheryl Boyd Zimmerman is a Professor at California State University, Fullerton. She specializes in second-language vocabulary acquisition, an area in which she is widely published. She teaches graduate courses on second-language acquisition, culture, vocabulary, and the fundamentals of TESOL and is a frequent invited speaker on topics related to vocabulary teaching and learning. She is the author of *Word Knowledge: A Vocabulary Teacher's Handbook* and Series Director of *Inside Reading*, *Inside Writing*, and *Inside Listening and Speaking*, all published by Oxford University Press.

ASSESSMENT

Lawrence J. Zwier holds an M.A. in TESL from the University of Minnesota. He is currently the Associate Director for Curriculum Development at the English Language Center at Michigan State University in East Lansing. He has taught ESL/EFL in the United States, Saudi Arabia, Malaysia, Japan, and Singapore.

HOW TO USE iQ ONLINE

iQ ONLINE extends your learning beyond the classroom. This online content is specifically designed for you! *iQ Online* gives you flexible access to essential content.

Activities include
• Additional **practice** and support
• **Videos**—watch anytime, anywhere
• **Online tests** assigned by your teacher.

Progress reports show what skills you have learned and where you still need more practice.

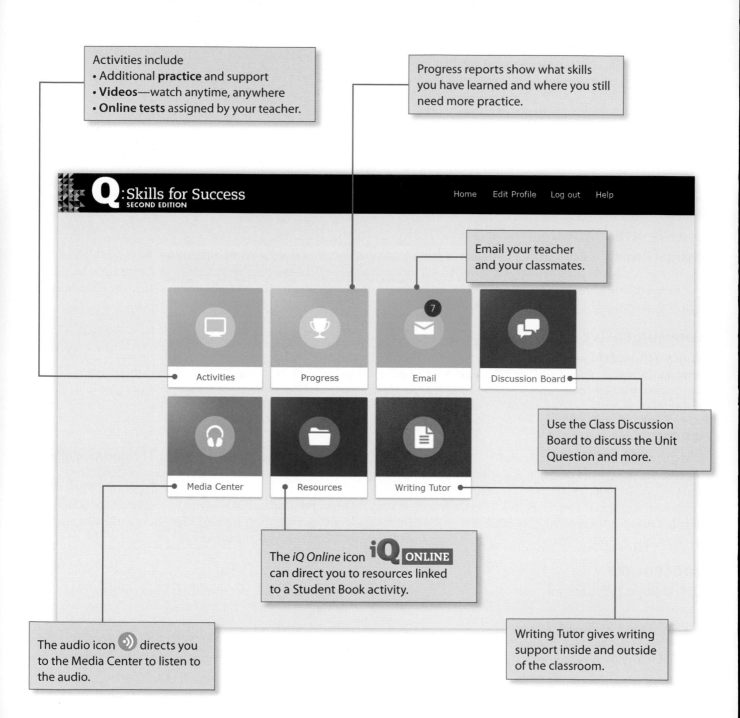

Email your teacher and your classmates.

Use the Class Discussion Board to discuss the Unit Question and more.

The *iQ Online* icon can direct you to resources linked to a Student Book activity.

The audio icon directs you to the Media Center to listen to the audio.

Writing Tutor gives writing support inside and outside of the classroom.

SEE THE INSIDE FRONT COVER FOR HOW TO REGISTER FOR *iQ ONLINE* FOR THE FIRST TIME.

Take Control of Your Learning

You have the choice of where and how you complete the activities. Access your activities and view your progress at any time.

Your teacher may

- assign *iQ Online* as homework,
- do the activities with you in class, or
- let you complete the activities at a pace that is right for you.

iQ Online makes it easy to access everything you need.

Set Clear Goals

STEP 1 If it is your first time, look through the site. See what learning opportunities are available.

STEP 2 The Student Book provides the framework and purpose for each online activity. Before going online, notice the goal of the exercises you are going to do.

STEP 3 Stay on top of your work, following the teacher's instructions.

STEP 4 Use *iQ Online* for review. You can use the materials any time. It is easy for you to do follow-up activities when you have missed a class or want to review.

Manage Your Progress

The activities in *iQ Online* are designed for you to work independently. You can become a confident learner by monitoring your progress and reviewing the activities at your own pace. You may already be used to working online, but if you are not, go to your teacher for guidance.

Check 'View Reports' to monitor your progress. The reports let you track your own progress at a glance. Think about your own performance and set new goals that are right for you, following the teacher's instructions.

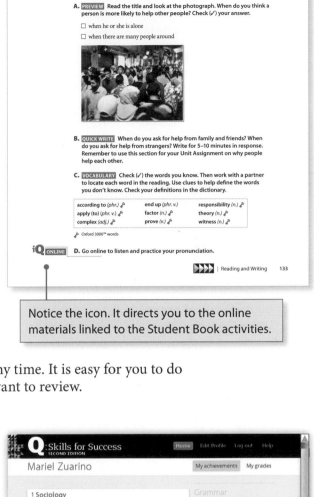

Notice the icon. It directs you to the online materials linked to the Student Book activities.

iQ Online is a research-based solution specifically designed for English language learners that extends learning beyond the classroom. I hope these steps help you make the most of this essential content.

C. N. Hemmi

Chantal Hemmi, EdD TEFL
Center for Language Education and Research
Sophia University, Japan

213

🔊 *Q: Skills for Success Second Edition* audio can be found in the Media Center.

Follow these steps:

Step 1: Go to iQOnlinePractice.com.

Step 2: Click on the Media Center icon. 🔼

Step 3: Choose to stream or download ⬇ the audio file you select. Not all audio files are available for download.

Class Audio

Unit	Page	Listen	Download
Unit 1			
1	3	The Q Classroom	⬇
1	6	Work With the Reading	⬇
1	13	Work With the Reading	⬇
Unit 2			
2	28	The Q Classroom	⬇
2	32	Work With the Reading	⬇
2	38	Work With the Reading	⬇
Unit 3			
3	55	The Q Classroom	⬇
3	58	Work With the Reading	⬇
3	65	Work With the Reading	

Back

Unit	Activity	Track File Name
Unit 1	The Q Classroom, p. 3	Q2e_03_RW_U01_ Q_Classroom.mp3
	Work With the Reading, p. 6	Q2e_03_RW_U01_ Reading1.mp3
	Work With the Reading, p. 13	Q2e_03_RW_U01_Reading2.mp3
Unit 2	The Q Classroom, p. 28	Q2e_03_RW_U02_Q_Classroom.mp3
	Work With the Reading, p.32	Q2e_03_RW_U02_Reading1.mp3
	Work With the Reading, p.38	Q2e_03_RW_U02_Reading2.mp3
Unit 3	The Q Classroom, p. 55	Q2e_03_RW_U03_Q_Classroom.mp3
	Work With the Reading, p.58	Q2e_03_RW_U03_Reading1.mp3
	Work With the Reading, p. 65	Q2e_03_RW_U03_Reading2.mp3
Unit 4	The Q Classroom, p. 81	Q2e_03_RW_U04_Q_Classroom.mp3
	Work With the Reading, p. 84	Q2e_03_RW_U04_Reading1.mp3
	Work With the Reading, p. 91	Q2e_03_RW_U04_Reading2.mp3
Unit 5	The Q Classroom, p. 105	Q2e_03_RW_U05_Q_Classroom.mp3
	Work With the Reading, p. 108	Q2e_03_RW_U05_Reading1.mp3
	Work With the Reading, p. 116	Q2e_03_RW_U05_Reading2.mp3
Unit 6	The Q Classroom, p. 130	Q2e_03_RW_U06_Q_Classroom.mp3
	Work With the Reading, p. 134	Q2e_03_RW_U06_Reading1.mp3
	Work With the Reading, p. 142	Q2e_03_RW_U06_Reading2.mp3
Unit 7	The Q Classroom, p. 158	Q2e_03_RW_U07_Q_Classroom.mp3
	Work With the Reading, p. 162	Q2e_03_RW_U07_Reading1.mp3
	Work With the Reading, p. 169	Q2e_03_RW_U07_Reading2.mp3
Unit 8	The Q Classroom, p. 187	Q2e_03_RW_U08_Q_Classroom.mp3
	Work With the Reading, p. 190	Q2e_03_RW_U08_Reading1.mp3
	Work With the Reading, p. 195	Q2e_03_RW_U08_Reading2.mp3

🔑 The keywords of the **Oxford 3000™** have been carefully selected by a group of language experts and experienced teachers as the words which should receive priority in vocabulary study because of their importance and usefulness.

AWL **The Academic Word List** is the most principled and widely accepted list of academic words. Averil Coxhead gathered information from academic materials across the academic disciplines to create this word list.

The Common European Framework of Reference for Languages (CEFR) provides a basic description of what language learners have to do to use language effectively. The system contains 6 reference levels: **A1, A2, B1, B2, C1, C2.** CEFR leveling provided by the Word Family Framework, created by Richard West and published by the British Council. http://www.learnenglish.org.uk/wff/

UNIT 1

accomplishment *(n.)*, B2
appreciate *(v.)* 🔑 AWL , A2
confidence *(n.)* 🔑, B1
consider *(v.)* 🔑, A1
demonstrate *(v.)* 🔑 AWL , A2
effective *(adj.)* 🔑, A1
exaggerate *(v.)* 🔑, C1
expect *(v.)* 🔑, B1
impress *(v.)* 🔑, B1
lead to *(phr. v.)* 🔑, B2
maintain *(v.)* 🔑 AWL , A1
offensive *(adj.)* 🔑, B1
professional *(adj.)* 🔑 AWL , A1
punctual *(adj.)*, B1
research *(n.)* 🔑 AWL , B1
responsible *(adj.)* 🔑, A1
select *(v.)* 🔑 AWL , B1
slang *(n.)*, C1
stranger *(n.)* 🔑, B1
weakness *(n.)* 🔑, B1

UNIT 2

at risk *(phr.)*, B2
balanced *(adj.)*, B2
be made up of *(phr. v.)*, B1
concept *(n.)* 🔑 AWL , A1
consume *(v.)* AWL , B2

cuisine *(n.)*, C1
identify *(v.)* 🔑 AWL , A1
influence *(v.)* 🔑, A2
likely *(adj.)* 🔑, B1
method *(n.)* 🔑 AWL , B1
portion *(n.)* AWL , B2
practice *(n.)* 🔑, A1
principle *(n.)* 🔑 AWL , B1
property *(n.)* 🔑, B1
region *(n.)* 🔑 AWL , B1
recognize *(v.)* 🔑, B1
sensitive *(adj.)* 🔑, B1
system *(n.)* 🔑, A1
typically *(adv.)* 🔑, B1

UNIT 3

benefit *(n.)* 🔑 AWL , B1
confession *(n.)*, B2
data *(n.)* 🔑 AWL , A1
discover *(v.)* 🔑, B1
eventually *(adv.)* 🔑 AWL , A1
experiment *(n.)* 🔑, B1
lifestyle *(n.)*, B2
limitation *(n.)*, C1
manufacturer *(n.)* 🔑, B1
obey *(v.)* 🔑, A2
obstacle *(n.)*, C1
occasion *(n.)* 🔑, A2

occur *(v.)* 🔑 AWL , A1
rare *(adj.)* 🔑, B1
regret *(v.)* 🔑, B1
respond *(v.)* 🔑 AWL , B1
sense *(v.)* 🔑, A1
survive *(v.)* 🔑 AWL , A1

UNIT 4

annoying *(adj.)* 🔑, B1
annual *(adj.)* 🔑 AWL , B1
anticipation *(n.)* AWL , C2
appealing *(adj.)*, B2
appear *(v.)* 🔑, B1
broadcasting *(n.)*, B2
donation *(n.)*, B2
entertain *(v.)* 🔑, B1
exposure *(n.)*, C1
claim *(v.)* 🔑, A1
come close to *(phr. v.)*, C1
critic *(n.)* 🔑, B1
deceptive *(adj.)*, C2
figure out *(phr. v.)*, B2
hire *(v.)* 🔑, A2
particularly *(adv.)* 🔑, B1
memorable *(adj.)*, B2
support *(v.)* 🔑, B1
surrounding *(adj.)* 🔑, B2

UNIT 5

aspect *(n.)* 🔑 AWL, A1
bravely *(adv.)*, B1
challenge *(n.)* 🔑 AWL, B1
conquer *(v.)*, C1
determined *(adj.)* 🔑, B2
distinctive *(adj.)* AWL, C1
earn *(v.)* 🔑, A2
goal *(n.)* 🔑 AWL, B1
mental *(adj.)* 🔑 AWL, A2
notable *(adj.)*, C1
perceive *(v.)* AWL, C1
precaution *(n.)*, C1
pursuit *(n.)* AWL, C2
role *(n.)* 🔑 AWL, A2
significant *(adj.)* 🔑 AWL, A1
tolerance *(n.)*, C2
trait *(n.)*, C2
ultimate *(adj.)* 🔑 AWL, B1
vivid *(adj.)*, B2

UNIT 6

according to *(phr.)* 🔑, A1
altruistic *(adj.)*, C2
apply to *(phr. v.)* 🔑, B1
barely *(adv.)* 🔑, B1
bring about *(phr. v.)*, B2
compassionate *(adj.)*, C2
complex *(adj.)* 🔑 AWL, A2
end up *(phr. v.)*, B1
factor *(n.)* 🔑 AWL, A1
hypothesize *(v.)* AWL, B2
initial *(adj.)* 🔑 AWL, A2
prove *(v.)* 🔑, A1
rely on *(phr. v.)* 🔑 AWL, A2

responsibility *(n.)* 🔑, A1
subject *(n.)* 🔑, B1
theory *(n.)* 🔑 AWL, A1
witness *(n.)* 🔑, B1

UNIT 7

adjustment *(n.)* AWL, B1
aim *(v.)* 🔑, B1
ambition *(n.)* 🔑, B1
approach *(n.)* 🔑 AWL, A1
assumption *(n.)* AWL, C1
attend *(v.)* 🔑, B1
commitment *(n.)* 🔑 AWL, A2
distribute *(v.)* 🔑 AWL, B1
enable *(v.)* 🔑 AWL, A1
encourage *(v.)* 🔑, B1
expand *(v.)* 🔑 AWL, A2
extremely *(adv.)* 🔑, B1
generosity *(n.)*, B2
impact *(n.)* 🔑 AWL, B1
inspire *(v.)*, B1
measurable *(adj.)*, B2
network *(n.)* 🔑 AWL, B2
owe *(v.)* 🔑, B1
proud *(adj.)* 🔑, B1
transition *(n.)* 🔑, B1

UNIT 8

aggressively *(adv.)*, B2
assured *(adj.)* AWL, C2
dedication *(n.)*, C1
demanding *(adj.)*, B2
dependable *(adj.)*, B1
due to *(prep.)* 🔑, B1
exception *(n.)* 🔑, B1

expansion *(n.)* AWL, B1
image *(n.)* 🔑 AWL, B1
invest *(v.)* 🔑 AWL, B1
logo *(n.)*, B1
market *(n.)* 🔑, A2
motion *(n.)* 🔑, A2
profits *(n.)* 🔑, C2
recover *(v.)* 🔑 AWL, A2
sign *(n.)* 🔑, A2
sponsor *(v.)*, B2
stability *(n.)* AWL, C1
trend *(n.)* 🔑 AWL, B1